A LITERARY READER

Asian
American
WRITERS

Los Gatos High School

nextext

DONATION

BC# T35891

Table of Contents

*Throughout the reader, vocabulary words appear in boldface
type and are footnoted. Specialized or technical words and phrases
appear in lightface type and are footnoted.*

Arriving in America

Immigration Blues

BY ANONYMOUS CHINESE IMMIGRANTS

*To many impoverished farmers and laborers from South China,
California's 1848 Gold Rush held out the promise of fortunes
to be made. By 1850, thousands were coming to the United States,
or Jinshan, which means "Gold Mountain" in Chinese. After the
Chinese Exclusion Act of 1882, however, Chinese laborers arriving
in San Francisco could no longer get off the boat and look for
work. The U.S. Immigration Service detained immigrants on Angel
Island in San Francisco Bay. Many remained there for weeks,
months, or even a year. Frustrated, angry, and occasionally suicidal,
some of the men scribbled poems on the wooden walls of the
barracks. These five poems, from* Songs of Gold Mountain *(1987),
translated by Marlon K. Hom, poignantly recount the immigrants'
dreams of a better life in America and the bitter reality they
encountered upon arrival.*

I

As soon as it is announced
    the ship has reached America:
I burst out cheering,
    I have found precious pearls.

How can I bear the detention upon arrival,
Doctors and immigration officials refusing to let me go?
All the abuse—
I can't describe it with a pen.
I'm held captive in a wooden barrack, like King Wen[1]
    in Youli:
No end to the misery and sadness in my heart.

II

At home I was in poverty,
    constantly worried about firewood and rice.
I borrowed money
    to come to Gold Mountain.[2]
Immigration officers cross-examined me;
    no way could I get through.
Deported to this island,
    like a convicted criminal.
Here—
Mournful sighs fill the gloomy room.
A nation weak; her people often humiliated
Like animals, tortured and destroyed at others'
    whim.

III

The wooden cell is like a steel barrel.
Firmly shut, not even a breeze can filter through.
Over a hundred cruel laws, hard to list them all;
Ten thousand grievances, all from the tortures day and
    night.
Worry, and more worry—
How can I sleep in peace or eat at ease?

---

[1] King Wen—first ruler of the Chinese Zhou dynasty (1122 B.C.–256 B.C.)
He was held in Youli by a rival Shang dynasty ruler.

[2] Gold Mountain—California. At the time of the Gold Rush, there was a
political upheaval and widespread poverty and famine in southeastern China.
Shipowners advertised the benefits of the "golden hills" of California to
desperate men, who emigrated by the thousands.

There isn't a cangue,[3] but the hidden punishment is just
    as weighty.
Tears soak my clothes; frustration fills my bosom.

IV

So, liberty is your national principle;
Why do you practice **autocracy**?[4]
You don't uphold justice, you Americans,
You detain me in prison, guard me closely.
Your officials are wolves and tigers,
All ruthless, all wanting to bite me.
An innocent man implicated, such an injustice!
When can I get out of this prison and free my mind?

V

Fellow countrymen, four hundred million strong;
Many are great, with exceptional talents.
We want to come to the Flowery Flag Nation[5] but are
    barred;
The Golden Gate[6] firmly locked, without even a crack
    to crawl through.
This moment—
Truly deplorable is the imprisonment.
Our hearts ache in pain and shame;
Though talented, how can we put on wings and fly
    past the barbarians?

---

[3] cangue—Chinese device used to punish petty criminals. It consisted of a wooden yoke that enclosed both the head and hands.

[4] **autocracy**—a system of government in which one person has unlimited powers.

[5] Flowery Flag Nation—United States, so called because of the graphic design of the flag.

[6] Golden Gate—channel connecting San Francisco Bay with the Pacific Ocean. The poet sees the Golden Gate, traditionally viewed as a doorway to the promise and wealth of California, as closed to his countrymen.

QUESTIONS TO CONSIDER

1. What words would you use to describe the tone of these poems, and which poem do you find the most memorable?

2. What do these immigrants seem to find the most upsetting, and why?

3. How do these poets use figures of speech to communicate their feelings?

4. What first impressions do these immigrants have of the United States, and how do these impressions match their expectations?

Angel Island

BY SHAWN WONG

Shawn Wong (1949–   ), professor of creative writing at the University of Washington, published American Knees *(1995) and edited* The Literary Mosaic: An Anthology of Asian-American Literature *(1995). He received the Pacific Northwest Booksellers Award and a Washington State Governor's Writers Day Award for his novel,* Homebase *(1979), in which the following selection appears.*

In Homebase, *the first-person narrator is sometimes Rainsford Chan, a fourth-generation Chinese American growing up during the 1950s and 1960s, and sometimes Chan's immigrant ancestors. His great-grandfather was the first-generation Chan to settle in America. He had sent his son, Rainsford Chan's grandfather, to China "for safety" and for his education. But after the great-grandfather's death, the grandfather returns to America. Here Chan assumes his grandfather's voice to describe his impressions and feelings about Angel Island and the interrogation by immigration officials.*

Once inside, you will see that the room is lit with bare bulbs hung from the ceiling. You will see that the room is filled with men, women, and children. There are two lines—men and young boys in one and women and a few very young children in the other. An officer stands between the two lines. Behind a large counter there is an officer for each line. There is some shuffling but no talking except for the two officers behind the counter. You will see that we are dressed in drab jackets, some men are wearing long coats with black pants underneath, others are wearing regular work clothes, and many are wearing flat brim black hats.

You will know why you're standing in line with me. I am my grandfather come back to America after having been raised in China. My father is dead so I've had to assume someone else's name and family in order to legally enter the country. All this information about my new family has been memorized. All my sons after me will have my **assumed**[1] name.

I was not allowed to ever leave the building, even to go outside. Husbands were not allowed to see their wives or children, who were kept in another part of the building. We ate in different shifts. There were riots in the mess hall and the main building. We had given up everything to come to this country. Many were former citizens. If you run your fingers across the walls at night in the dark, your fingers will be filled with the splinters of poems carved into the walls. Maybe there is a dim light to help see what your fingers feel. But you can only read, "Staying on this island, my sorrow increases with the days/my face is growing **sallow**[2] and body is getting thin," before your fingers give out following the grooves and gouges of the characters.

Sometimes the morning will show you someone has hung themselves in the night, someone who could no longer bear the waiting, or the interrogation, or failing the interrogation—someone waiting to be sent back to China. Everyone knows how to hang yourself. There are no nails or hooks high enough to hang a piece of cloth

---

[1] **assumed**—adopted.

[2] **sallow**—a sickly yellowish-green.

from and leap from a stool to a quick death. There is only one way—to tie your piece of cloth on one of those big nails about four and a half feet off the floor, lean against the wall to brace yourself, and bend your knees and hold them up off the floor. Then your bones will be collected and placed on the open seas.

I have memorized someone else's family history, taken someone else's name, and suppressed everything that I have **chronicled**[3] for myself. The questions begin in the Interrogation Room. It is a room blocked off from the light. The windows are painted black. One immigration officer has a list of questions in his hand and the other has a file folder in front of him with the data given by relatives years ago.

Question: How large is your village?

Answer: It has fifty houses.

Question: How many rows of houses are there?

Answer: Ten rows.

Question: Which way does the village face and where is the head?

Answer: It faces east and the head is south.

Question: Where is your house located?

Answer: Second house, third row, counting from the south.

Question: Do you know who lived in that house before your family?

Answer: I do not remember.

Question: How many houses in your row?

Answer: Five.

Question: Do all of the houses in your row touch each other?

Answer: None of them do.

Question: How far apart are they?

Answer: About six feet.

---

[3] **chronicled**—described; recorded.

Question: What were the sleeping arrangements in your house when you were last in China?

Answer: My mother, all my brothers, and I occupied the south bedroom.

Question: How many beds are in the south bedroom?

Answer: Sometimes two, and sometimes three.

Question: Please explain that statement.

Answer: When the weather gets warm, we use three.

Question: How many steps lead to your front door?

Answer: None.

Question: Is there a clock in your house?

Answer: Yes.

Question: Describe it.

Answer: It is wood on the outside. It is brass with a white porcelain[4] face. It has brass numbers.

Question: Where did your mother buy **provisions**?[5]

Answer: She buys at the Tin Wo Market.

Question: How far and in what direction is that from your village?

Answer: One or two lis[6] west.

Question: How many of your brothers have attended school?

Answer: All my brothers.

Question: Did they attend the same school with you?

Answer: Yes.

Question: When did your youngest brother start school?

Answer: The beginning of this year.

Question: When did your oldest brother start school?

Answer: When he was eleven years old.

Question: When did you quit school?

Answer: I attended school for six months this year, then I quit.

---

[4] porcelain—hard, white, semitransparent ceramic ware (like china).

[5] **provisions**—supplies; groceries.

[6] one or two lis—about one-third to two-thirds of a mile.

Question: Who told you to quit?

Answer: My mother. She told me to prepare myself to go to the United States.

Question: When did you first learn that you were to come to the United States of America?

Answer: About the time my mother told me to quit school.

The officer asking the questions stops for a moment. He puts down the paper he's been reading from and draws out a tobacco pouch and begins to roll a cigarette for himself. He rises from his chair and goes to the window. He licks his cigarette and draws a match out from his pocket and lights his cigarette. The second officer has stopped writing whatever he was writing and puts down his pencil. The first one begins scraping the black paint from a small section of the window. He pulls out his pocket knife, unfolds it, and continues scraping until he has a small peephole. "It's a nice day outside," he says to no one. . . .

QUESTIONS TO CONSIDER

1. What did the narrator have to give up to enter the United States? Why?

2. How would you describe the atmosphere of the Interrogation Room, the demeanor of the officials, and the feelings of the person telling the story?

3. Why do you think the officials ask the questions they do? What questions do you think would be relevant to ask someone in this situation?

4. What do the author's style, tone, and use of language bring to this story that a strict reporting of someone's entry at Angel Island might not provide?

5. Why do you think Wong chose to have the main character speak through his grandfather's voice rather than tell the story in third person?

from

America Is in the Heart

BY CARLOS BULOSAN

Writer and poet Carlos Bulosan (c. 1911–1956) came to the United States from the Philippines at the age of sixteen. He survived a difficult ocean crossing to arrive in Seattle in the middle of the Depression. Jobs were scarce, which increased the hatred, discrimination, and exploitation directed toward many new arrivals. For years Bulosan worked as a migrant worker and dishwasher, and later became a radical labor organizer and writer for a union newspaper. Bulosan wrote stories, essays, poems, correspondence, and many books. His first book of fiction, The Laughter of My Father, *became a bestseller during World War II. Bulosan's autobiography,* America Is in the Heart: A Personal History *(1946), is considered a classic in Asian-American literature, documenting the collective life of thousands of Filipino immigrants in the United States. In the following excerpt, Bulosan relates the details of his first two harrowing days in the United States.*

We arrived in Seattle on a June day. My first sight of approaching land was an **exhilarating**[1] experience. Everything seemed native and promising to me. It was like coming home after a long voyage, although as yet I had no home in this city. Everything seemed familiar and kind—the white faces of the buildings melting in the soft afternoon sun, the gray contours of the surrounding valleys that seemed to vanish in the last **periphery**[2] of light. With a sudden surge of joy, I knew that I must find a home in this new land.

I had only twenty cents left, not even enough to take me to Chinatown where, I had been informed, a Filipino hotel and two restaurants were located. Fortunately two oldtimers put me in a car with four others, and took us to a hotel on King Street, the heart of Filipino life in Seattle. Marcelo, who was also in the car, had a cousin named Elias who came to our room with another old-timer. Elias and his unknown friend persuaded my companions to play a strange kind of card game. In a little while Elias got up and touched his friend suggestively; then they disappeared and we never saw them again.

It was only when our two countrymen had left that my companions realized what happened. They had taken all the money. Marcelo asked me if I had any money. I gave him my twenty cents. After collecting a few more cents from the others, he went downstairs and when he came back he told us that he had telegraphed for money to his brother in California.

All night we waited for the money to come, hungry and afraid to go out in the street. Outside we could hear shouting and singing; then a woman screamed lustily in one of the rooms down the hall. Across from our hotel a jazz band was playing noisily; it went on until dawn. But in the morning a telegram came to Marcelo which said:

---

[1] **exhilarating**—invigorating; stimulating; energizing.

[2] **periphery**—outer region or area.

YOUR BROTHER DIED AUTOMOBILE
ACCIDENT LAST WEEK

Marcelo looked at us and began to cry. His anguish stirred an aching fear in me. I knelt on the floor looking for my suitcase under the bed. I knew that I had to go out now—alone. I put the suitcase on my shoulder and walked toward the door, stopping for a moment to look back at my friends who were still standing silently around Marcelo. Suddenly a man came into the room and announced that he was the **proprietor.**[3]

"Well, boys," he said, looking at our suitcases, "where is the rent?"

"We have no money, sir," I said, trying to impress him with my politeness.

"That is too bad," he said quickly, glancing **furtively**[4] at our suitcases again. "That is just too bad." He walked outside and went down the hall. He came back with a short, fat Filipino, who looked at us stupidly with his dull, small eyes, and spat his cigar out of the window.

"There they are, Jake," said the proprietor.

Jake looked disappointed. "They are too young," he said.

"You can break them in, Jake," said the proprietor.

"They will be sending babies next," Jake said.

"You can break them in, can't you, Jake?" the proprietor pleaded. "This is not the first time you have broken babies in. You have done it in the sugar plantations in Hawaii, Jake!"

"Hell!" Jake said, striding across the room to the proprietor. He pulled a fat roll of bills from his pocket and gave twenty-five dollars to the proprietor. Then he

---

[3] **proprietor**—owner; person in charge.
[4] **furtively**—quickly and secretly.

turned to us and said, "All right, Pinoys,[5] you are working for me now. Get your hats and follow me."

We were too frightened to hesitate. When we lifted our suitcases the proprietor ordered us not to touch them.

"I'll take care of them until you come back from Alaska," he said. "Good fishing, boys!"

In this way we were sold for five dollars each to work in the fish canneries in Alaska, by a Visayan from the island of Leyte to an Ilocano[6] from the province of La Union. Both were oldtimers; both were tough. They **exploited**[7] young immigrants until one of them, the hotel proprietor, was shot dead by an unknown assailant. We were forced to sign a paper which stated that each of us owed the contractor twenty dollars for bedding and another twenty for luxuries. What the luxuries were, I have never found out. The contractor turned out to be a tall, heavy-set, dark Filipino, who came to the small hold of the boat barking at us like a dog. He was drunk and saliva was running down his shirt.

"And get this, you devils!" he shouted at us. "You will never come back alive if you don't do what I say!"

It was the beginning of my life in America, the beginning of a long flight that carried me down the years, fighting desperately to find peace in some corner of life.

---

[5] Pinoys— people from the Philippine Islands, Filipinos.

[6] Visayans are the largest native group in the Philippines; Ilocanos are another native group.

[7] **exploited**—took advantage of.

QUESTIONS TO CONSIDER

1. What are Bulosan's first impressions of the United States?

2. Why do you think Marcelo's brother's death "stirred an aching fear" in Bulosan?

3. What happened to Bulosan? Why?

4. What do you think the responsibility of the United States government and its citizens should be toward the treatment of newcomers from other countries?

Of Luggage and Shoes

BY THUY DINH

Thuy Dinh, a U.S. government lawyer based in Washington D.C., was born in Vietnam in 1962. In 1975, at the age of thirteen, Thuy Dinh and her family fled Vietnam to settle in the United States. They had been living with her grandfather, who worked for American military advisers, while her father was in prison for writing subversive material in the newspaper. As the defeat of the South Vietnamese government was imminent, her grandfather planned the family's departure. Dinh relates the preparations for leaving the capital city, Saigon, and the hectic, uncertain days that followed as they made their way toward what Thuy imagined would be Paradise. "Of Luggage and Shoes" was written for the spring 1991 issue of Amerasia.

When I was little I used to think of America as a sort of unattainable Paradise. America was grander than France, even grander than the whole of Europe, and summed up that exotic word "abroad." I knew that only smart or really rich people could ever go to America. But as a child I did not understand or believe in my intellect.

Also, my parents were not **manifestly**[1] rich. I thought I could never go to Paradise, but was doomed to get married early, have numerous children and live a life full of cooking and embroidery.

In April of 1975, we were given the opportunity to go to America as refugees of a soon-to-be extinct republic. . . .

During the preparation stage my grandfather was deeply concerned about shoes. He told my mother: "I heard that shoes were very expensive in America, so perhaps you may want to take the children to the shoe store or the cobbler to get their shoes fitted. Whatever we can do now, it will save time and money later on."

In Saigon all kinds of shoes were affordable. So, convinced by my grandfather's advice, my mother took us shopping. Each of my younger brothers got a pair of burgundy penny loafers, with a round, shiny silver buckle on the side. They also got new dress shirts, jackets, and slacks to go with their new shoes. I got a pair of sling-backed, pink leather pumps with black patent platform heels. . . .

For luggage, my grandfather told us, we each could only bring two bags. I stuffed into my knapsacks my pink shoes, my favorite Sunday dress and my new bell-bottom pants, along with my best written essays from seventh-grade composition class, and bags of chopsticks and rusty silverware from my grandmother's kitchen cabinet. I thought they would come in handy if we had to eat on the road. My younger sister was less practical. She stuffed into her plastic carry-on a huge comic book that she recently received for her eighth birthday. Later on my mother took out the essay and the chopsticks and silverware from my bags. She also persuaded my sister to leave behind her comic book. "Those things are not fit for travel," she said.

---

[1] **manifestly**—obviously.

I realized that whether or not something could be brought along had less to do with its appropriateness as a thing, but a lot more to do with your order in the world. My grandfather, as the highest authority in the house, could bring along with him his *dan tranh*, a five-foot-long amber-colored, mahogany-trimmed, classical Vietnamese string instrument . . . . He has not touched the instrument ever since we came to the United States.

We led the live-in help to believe that we were getting ready for a trip to the country. . . .

One of the help, an exuberant country girl about seventeen, jumped for her freedom as she waved good-bye. . . . We had on our Sunday best. It was Easter Sunday, April 20, 1975.

The next day, April 21, we boarded an American military aircraft carrier and headed toward Clark Air Base, the Philippines. It was our first stop on the voyage to Paradise. . . .

We stayed on mattresses, in a huge gymnasium within the air base. For the first time in my life I was exposed to "communal living." It was not comfortable or pleasant. I did not like to see naked flesh in the women's washroom in the morning, or sleep side by side with other bodies in a big, foreign, depersonalized space. It was accidental, grand-scale camping. Ever hopeful, I projected my thought toward our next stop on the voyage. Perhaps things would get better as we got closer to America. But time did not seem to pass. . . .

I befriended a few people whose mattresses were across from ours. There was Kim, a gum-snapping Vietnamese woman married to an American G.I., who taught me that "Coke" is a shortened version of Coca-Cola. I did not believe her. . . .

I also had another friend, a girl my own age named Trinh who left Vietnam with her father. She was proud of the fact that she wore sneakers: "My dad bought me the sneakers. He said everyone wears sneakers in America for comfort."

I did not believe her. My pink heels were much more stylish than her masculine-looking sneakers. They were now a little worn on the heels and scuff-toed. I had worn them every day since we left. I closed my eyes, dreaming of crossing a wide boulevard in America in my pink shoes, walking, or floating, toward a slope-edged, brightly lit skyscraper. I refused the proletarian notion[2] of sneakers.

After a few days in Clark Air Base, we left the Philippines for Guam Island. But contrary to my expectations, Guam was much more depressing than the Philippines. We were not anywhere near the beach or the palm trees. Instead we were shuffled into a long, narrow barracks that looked like a hospital wing. We did not have "men" and "women" bathing areas, but both sexes, by rotation, shared one wet area shielded by an off-white plastic curtain. My mother thought the alley behind this bathing area was haunted.

At night, the G.I.s would show animated shorts[3] in the open area in the front of the barracks. We never missed a showing. Arriving early, my siblings and I would take up a whole bench. So there we would sit midway between Vietnam and the New World, with a full moon above us, and a huge white screen in front of us, watching *Bugs Bunny* and *The Road Runner*. Sometimes there would be *Popeye the Sailor Man*, or Dr. Seuss' *The Cat in the Hat*. Looking back, those animated shorts represented the only constant vision of America. Other **preconceived notions**,[4] like fragments in a kaleidoscope, changed and shifted, distorted by experience as time passed on.

---

[2] proletarian notion—lower-class idea.

[3] animated shorts—cartoons.

[4] **preconceived notions**—concepts or ideas formed before one has actual firsthand knowledge.

We stayed in Guam for about a week, but it seemed an eternity. Our clothing, new and stylish when we left, began to take on a dull thickish look. My brothers' penny loafers were now open at the toe parts. They looked like shy crocodile mouths. I had worn thin the leather soles of my pink shoes. I missed my composition essays that I almost got to bring on the trip. My sister missed her comic book. My mother missed my father and their life before the changes. My grandparents missed their whole past. Trinh still looked proud of the fact that her sneakers were in good condition.

One morning about the sixth day of our stay in Guam, my grandfather ran in from outside and said: "Well, that's it, Vietnam has been lost." He said it in an even tone, perhaps too shocked to embrace the reality of the situation. My mother looked at my grandmother. I looked at the steel bedpost, at nothing. At the back of the barrack someone started to cry. Then several others joined in. Several infants, scared by their elders' weeping, also began to bawl. We mourned for a nation that was turning fast into an **abstraction**.[5]

But the memories would come back, later on, more real than ever, years after I had learned American English beyond a simple "hello." Perhaps the nation did not become extinct, but evolved into something else **akin**[6] to the expatriate's collective awareness,[7] eternal, constant, yet a part of my own consciousness, a part of the Vietnamese I still speak to my parents. To be a refugee is not to avoid your **catastrophes**[8] but to face them head on, unflinching, the eyes not dazed by the intense whiteness of Paradise.

So with worn pink shoes, I entered the Promised Land.

---

[5] **abstraction**—not a part of concrete existence.

[6] **akin**—similar.

[7] **expatriate's collective awareness**—awareness, shared by others, of one who has left or been exiled from his or her native land.

[8] **catastrophes**—disasters.

QUESTIONS TO CONSIDER

1. What did the family members want to take with them when they left Vietnam? If you were in their situation, what would you want to take?

2. What is ironic about Dinh's attitude toward the girl who wears sneakers?

3. What do the pink shoes symbolize to Dinh?

4. What do you think Dinh means by the "intense whiteness of Paradise"?

Song of Calling Souls

(The Drowned Voices from the Golden Venture)

BY WANG PING

Born in Shanghai in 1957, Wang Ping left China for New York in 1985. She has had a book of short stories published, American Visa *(1995) and a novel,* Foreign Devil *(1996). Her poetry has appeared in many periodicals, including* The Best American Poetry 1993 *and* The Best American Poetry 1996. *"Song of Calling Souls," which appeared in* Sulfur, *is Ping's response to an incident that occurred in March 1994, when 286 illegal Chinese immigrants aboard the sinking* Golden Venture *jumped into the ocean. Ten people drowned and six unclaimed bodies were buried in a common grave in Paterson, New Jersey. This is Ping's prayer for peace for the six people buried there. Ping explains that there is nothing worse if you are Chinese than to become a yie qui, a stray ghost, someone who dies and is buried far from his or her home.*

So here we are
    in the evening darkness
    of Rose Hill Cemetery
gazing out from our ghosts
    like the homeless outside windows.
No moon,
    the spring not the spring of the old days.
Our bodies not ours,
    but only bodies rotting
    in the grave of *laofan.*[1]
We look at the sky
    the earth
    and the four directions.
The storm gathers in
    from all sides.
How shall we pass through this night?

The wind comes blowing.
    We six
in deep shadow
    stand at the end of time,
stand in the night
    that is not just an absence of light,
but a persistent voice,
    unsteady and formless,
hum of summer crickets.

Something wants to be said,
    even if our words
grasp the air in vain
    and nothing remains.
Our story has set a fact
    beyond fable
Our story
    has no beginning or end.

---

[1] *laofan*—prison.

"Home" we say,
and before we utter we utter the word,
our voices choke with longing:

The cliff of Fuzhou[2]
      studded with stiff pines.
The waters of Changle[3]
      shadowed in the sway of bamboo.
Sea and sky fused.
      Mystic fires along the shore.
Fishermen's dwellings everywhere

      How lovely!
      How familiar!

When dusk falls,
      faint seagull cries.
Blue smoke rises
      from red-tiled roofs.
Small boats offshore
      and fishhawks in silhouette.
Salty winds
      carrying the murmur of reeds.
Tide roads of the sea.

The scenes grow in memory,
scenes we lived day by day,
paying no mind:
    Generation after generation,
        nets cast into the lingering light,
        seeds planted in the morning mist.
    Fishing kept us out on the waves.
    Farming bound our women to the soil.

---

[2] Fuzhou—the capital of Fujian, a province on China's southeast coast.

[3] Changle—a seacoast county in Fujian province.

But at times
   we heard a voice, a promise,
      a golden dream.
Things seen and heard
   turned to confusion.
We pulled our boats onto shore,
   left our wives and children
   behind the mountain's shadow.

From village to village
   we bought and sold
anything at hand
   socks underwear suits and dresses gold even drugs
seven days a week
   three hundred sixty-five days a year
and not just for the money:
   the yearning for adventure
   ran deep in our veins.
We played hide-and-seek
   with the government and police.
When we got caught and lost all our earnings
   we called ourselves "Norman Bethune."[4]
If Mao[5] were still alive
   he'd have surely praised us
   as he did that Canadian doctor
   who gave his life
   helping us fight the Japanese ghosts.

---

[4] Norman Bethune was a Canadian doctor (1890–1939) who was the first to introduce the mobile blood bank to the battlefield. In 1938, he went to China to minister to the soldiers in Mao's army and died there of blood poisoning. He is revered by the Chinese almost as a saint.

[5] In 1949, after nearly four decades of working to establish a socialist society, Mao Zedong (1893–1976) became Chairman and principal architect of the communist government of the People's Republic of China.

We were glad
   to help build a "socialist" China
   with our illegal gains.
Anyway we had a good laugh
   over our losses.
Still, waves of desire
   rose daily,
this voice luring
   from the far side of the sea.
Not that we yearned for gold
   or worldly delights,
but this voice
   first muttering
            then roaring in our heads,

So in hope and fear we **fared.**[6]
   In tears we fared.
Mist spread a veil
   till ocean-bound.
Pinewood mirrored
   in deep green.
At the bottom of the *Golden Venture*
   we did not see our women weeping
   did not hear our children calling.
Only the cry
   "Kari, kari . . ."
of wild geese.

We sailed the ocean
   in the hold of the *Golden Venture*—
            pigs chickens dogs snakes,
   whatever it was they called us.
Our bodies not ours
   sold to the "snakeheads"[7] for the trip.

---

6 **fared**—got along; traveled.

7 "snakeheads"—Fujianese smugglers of illegal aliens, or "snakes," into New York.

You ask why we did this?
   Ask the geese why they migrate
         from north to south,
   why the eels swim thousands of miles
         to spawn in the sea.

Tides of desire
   rise for no reason.
So we fared with the faith
New York had more *fu*[8] than Fuzhou,
people there enjoyed "**perpetual**[9] happiness"
like the name of *Changle.*

So we sailed with the belief
   we could buy ourselves back for $30,000
      within three years.[10]
   Our hard work would bring freedom
      to the next generation.
   Our sons would be prosperous and happy,
      not like us, cursed
      by our own country, cursed
      by the "old barbarians."
   America needed our labor and skills
      as much as we needed its dream . . .

And here we are,
   hovering around this New Jersey cemetery.
Our bodies gone,
   but our blind souls still hanging
      like curtains soaked in rain.

         Our summer clothes so thin!
         So thin our dreams!

---

[8] *fu*—fortune; good luck.

[9] **perpetual**—everlasting; continual.

[10] They would work as indentured servants until they had paid back the price of their passage to the United States. Thirty thousand dollars was an outrageous price, far more than the most luxurious travel could cost.

Hovering,
    that dark night near Rockaway,[11]
our ship finally heaving into sight of New York.
In thirst and hunger we waited.
In fear and hope we waited
    to be lifted from the ship's hold
    and alight on the land of paradise
"Jump," we'd been told,
"once your feet touch American soil
    you'll be free."
In the dark rain we waited.
"Jump," someone shouted,
"the ship is sinking, the police are coming!"
So we jumped
    into the night
    into the raging sea,
our breasts smothered
    by foam and weeds,
our passions tangled,
    the breath beaten from our bodies
by despair and hate.

        Oh, we've sunk so low!
        We've sunk so low!

Only to rise again
    for clinging to wrongful things.
Easy to sink
    in the fire of desire.
Regret comes after the deed.
    Sorrow!
Sorrow stitched into the cloak of our souls.
Our former days now changed,
    leaving no trace.

---

[11] Rockaway—a beach town in New Jersey near where the *Golden Venture* went aground.

The distant mountain lies alone.
Shadows of the city so far away.
   Sorrow!
We can speak only in weeping,
memory nothing but white hair on the heart.
Condemned to wander,
lost among the roots of our six senses,
gazing at New York,
gazing homewards,
Fuzhou's mighty waves **roiling**[12] through the night,
bride in green unveiled in scarlet chamber,
lovers' pillows joined like Siamese twins.
   Who can avoid sorrow in this world?

Our legs lingering
   in the dew-drenched grass
here and there, still clinging.
This deep night,
   is it outside-this-world?
Our women and children
   still awaiting our return.
But here we are,
   nameless,
In life and after life,
   apart.
Our song is the crane
   calling in her cage
when she thinks of her young
   toward nightfall.
Will it reach Fuzhou and Changle
   and stir souls from their sleep?
On the boat
   we were close,
hundreds of us in the hold
   jammed in and in.

---

[12] **roiling**—moving turbulently.

Here we live even closer,
    six bodies in one hole,
the earth sifting into
    our common grave,
unmarked,
    no stone erected
then crumbling.
    Sands of the shore
may reach an end,
    but not our grief.

Home, oh go home!
    an empty wave.
Ten thousand voices,
    broadcast the pain.
    Please, oh please
call our names
            Chen Xinhan   Zhen Shimin
even if you can't
    say them right
            Lin Guoshui   Chen Dajie
even if you don't know
    our origin or age
            Wang Xin   Huang Changpin
Please, oh please
    call us.
Raise our shadows
    from the moss.
Be gentle
    as you call our names.
Do not wake us by force.
    But call us.
Do not let us fade
    from this place,
unlit and unfulfilled.

QUESTIONS TO CONSIDER

1. Why do the drowned voices want to tell their story?

2. Where do the men come from? What had they been doing before they took the sea voyage?

3. Why did they leave China?

4. What is "home" to the men? How and why does the idea of home change from the beginning to the end of the poem?

5. Why is it so important to the men that their names be called?

In the American Society

His Own Society

BY GISH JEN

*Chinese-American writer Gish Jen (1955–   ) changed her name
from Lillian to Gish, after the star of silent films, while she was in
high school. She has written two novels,* Typical American *(1991)
and* Mona in the Promised Land *(1996). This short story first
appeared in the* Southern Review *(1986) and is now part of Jen's
prizewinning short story collection,* Who's Irish? *(1999). In this
story, a Chinese-American family explores what it means to be part
of "American society."*

When my father took over the pancake house, it was
to send my little sister, Mona, and me to college. We
were only in junior high at the time, but my father
believed in getting a jump on things. "Those Americans
always saying it," he told us. "Smart guys thinking in

advance." My mother elaborated, explaining that businesses took bringing up, like children. They could take years to get going, she said, years.

In this case, though, we got rich right away. At two months, we were breaking even, and at four, those same hotcakes that could barely withstand the weight of butter and syrup were supporting our family with ease. My mother bought a station wagon with air conditioning, my father an oversized red vinyl recliner for the back room; and as time went on and the business continued to thrive, my father started to talk about his grandfather, and the village he had reigned over in China—things my father had never talked about when he worked for other people. He told us about the bags of rice his family would give out to the poor at New Year's, and about the people who came to beg, on their hands and knees, for his grandfather to **intercede**[1] for the more **wayward**[2] of their relatives. "Like that Godfather in the movie," he would tell us as, feet up, he distributed paychecks. Sometimes an employee would get two green envelopes instead of one, which meant that Jimmy needed a tooth pulled, say, or that Tiffany's husband was in the clinker again. "It's nothing, nothing," he would insist, sinking back into his chair. "Who else is going to taking care of you people?"

My mother would mostly just sigh about it. "Your father thinks this is China," she would say, and then she would go back to her mending. Once in a while, though, when my father had given away a particularly large sum, she would exclaim, outraged, "But this here is the U—S—of—A!"—this apparently having been what she used to tell immigrant stock boys when they came in late.

She didn't work at the supermarket anymore; but she had made it to the rank of manager before she left,

---

[1] **intercede**—step in; speak on behalf of.

[2] **wayward**—unruly; undisciplined.

and this had given her not only new words and phrases but new ideas about herself, and about America, and about what was what in general. She had opinions about how downtown should be zoned; she could pump her own gas and check her own oil; and for all that she used to chide Mona and me for being copycats, she herself was now interested in espadrilles,[3] and wallpaper, and, most recently, the town country club.

"So join already," said Mona, flicking a fly off her knee.

My mother **enumerated**[4] the problems as she sliced up a quarter round of watermelon. There was the cost. There was the waiting list. There was the fact that no one in our family played either tennis or golf.

"So what?" said Mona.

"It would be waste," said my mother.

"Me and Callie[5] can swim in the pool."

"Anyway, you need that recommendation letter from a member."

"Come *on*," said Mona. "Annie's mom'd write you a letter in a *sec*."

My mother's knife glinted in the early-summer sun. I spread some more newspaper on the picnic table.

"Plus, you have to eat there twice a month. You know what that means." My mother cut another, enormous slice of fruit.

"No, I *don't* know what that means," said Mona.

"It means Dad would have to wear a jacket, dummy," I said.

"Oh! Oh! Oh!" said Mona, clasping her hand to her breast. "Oh! Oh! Oh! Oh! Oh!"

We all laughed: My father had no use for nice clothes, and would wear only ten-year-old shirts, with grease-spotted pants, to show how little he cared what anyone thought.

---

[3] espadrilles—stylish flat sandals.

[4] **enumerated**—counted off or named one by one.

[5] Callie—the narrator, Mona's sister.

"Your father doesn't believe in joining the American society," said my mother. "He wants to have his own society."

"So go to dinner without him." Mona shot her seeds out in long arcs over the lawn. "Who cares what he thinks?"

But of course, we all did care, and knew my mother could not simply up and do as she pleased. For to embrace what my father embraced was to love him; and to embrace something else was to betray him.

He demanded a similar sort of loyalty of his workers, whom he treated more like servants than employees. Not in the beginning, of course. In the beginning, all he wanted was for them to keep on doing what they used to do, to which end he concentrated mostly on leaving them alone. As the months passed, though, he expected more and more of them, with the result that, for all his **largesse**,[6] he began to have trouble keeping help. The cooks and busboys complained that he asked them to fix radiators and trim hedges, not only at the restaurant but at our house; the waitresses, that he sent them on errands, and made them chauffeur him around. Our headwaitress, Gertrude, claimed that he once even asked her to scratch his back.

"It's not just the blacks don't believe in slavery," she said when she quit.

My father never quite registered her complaints, though, nor those of the others who left. Even after Eleanor quit, then Tiffany, and Gerald, and Jimmy, and even his best cook, Eureka Andy, for whom he had bought new glasses, he remained mostly convinced that the fault lay with them.

"All they understand is that assemble line," he **lamented**.[7] "Robots, they are. They want to be robots."

---

6 **largesse**—generosity.

7 **lamented**—moaned; cried.

There were occasions when the clear running truth seemed to **eddy**,[8] when he would pinch the vinyl of his chair up into little peaks and wonder if he was doing things right. But with time he would always smooth the peaks back down; and when business started to slide in the spring, he kept on like a horse in his ways.

By the summer, our dish boy was overwhelmed with scraping. It was no longer just the hash browns that people were leaving for trash, and the service was as bad as the food. The waitresses served up French pancakes instead of German, apple juice instead of orange. They spilled things on laps, on coats. On the Fourth of July, some **greenhorn**[9] sent an entire side of fries slaloming[10] down a lady's *Massif Central*.[11] Meanwhile, in the back room, my father labored through articles on the economy.

"What is housing starts?" he puzzled. "What is GNP?"[12]

Mona and I did what we could, filling in as busgirls and dishwashers, and, one afternoon, stuffing the comments box by the cashier's desk. That was Mona's idea. We rustled up a variety of pens and pencils, checked boxes for an hour, smeared the cards with coffee and grease, and waited. It took a few days for my father to notice that the box was full, and he didn't say anything about it for a few days more. Finally, though, he started to complain of fatigue; and then he began to complain that the staff was not what it could be. We encouraged him in this—pointing out, for instance, how many dishes got chipped. But in the end all that happened was that, for the first time since we took over the restaurant, my father got it into his head to fire someone. Skip, a

---

[8] **eddy**—go around in circles as in a whirlpool or vortex.

[9] **greenhorn**—inexperienced or immature person.

[10] slaloming—rapidly sliding like a skier on a zigzag course.

[11] *Massif Central*—mountainous plateau in south-central France. In this case, it refers to the woman's cleavage.

[12] GNP—abbreviation for "gross national product," an index of the economic health of the country.

skinny busboy who was saving up for a sports car, said nothing as my father mumbled on about the price of dishes. My father's hands shook as he wrote out the severance check[13] and once it was over, he spent the rest of the day napping in his chair.

Since it was going on midsummer, Skip wasn't easy to replace. We hung a sign in the window and advertised in the paper, but no one called the first week, and the person who called the second didn't show up for his interview. The third week, my father phoned Skip to see if he would come back, but a friend of his had already sold him a Corvette for cheap.

Finally, a Chinese guy named Booker turned up. He couldn't have been more than thirty, and was wearing a lighthearted seersucker suit, but he looked as though life had him pinned. His eyes were bloodshot and his chest sunken, and the muscles of his neck seemed to strain with the effort of holding his head up. In a single dry breath he told us that he had never bused tables but was willing to learn, and that he was on the lam[14] from the deportation authorities.

"I do not want to lie to you," he kept saying. He had come to the United States on a student visa but had run out of money and was now in a bind. He was **loath**[15] to go back to Taiwan, as it happened—he looked up at this point, to be sure my father wasn't pro-KMT[16]—but all he had was a phony Social Security card, and a willingness to absorb all blame, should anything untoward come to pass.

"I do not think, anyway, that it is against law to hire me, only to be me," he said, smiling faintly.

---

[13] severance check—final payment made to a worker upon termination of employment.

[14] on the lam—hiding from the law.

[15] **loath**—unwilling; reluctant.

[16] pro-KMT—a supporter of the nationalist Kuomintang party, the ruling political party on the Chinese island of Taiwan, in opposition to the Communists on the mainland.

Anyone else would have examined him on this, but my father conceived of laws as speed bumps rather than curbs. He wiped the counter with his sleeve, and told Booker to report the next morning.

"I will be good worker," said Booker.

"Good, " said my father.

"Anything you want me to do, I will do."

My father nodded.

Booker seemed to sink into himself for a moment. "Thank you," he said finally. "I am appreciate your help. I am very, very appreciate for everything."

My father looked at him. "Did you eat today?" he asked in Mandarin.[17]

Booker pulled at the hem of his jacket.

"Sit down," said my father. "Please, have a seat."

My father didn't tell my mother about Booker, and my mother didn't tell my father about the country club. She would never have applied, except that Mona, while over at Annie's, had let it drop that our mother wanted to join. Mrs. Lardner came by the very next day.

"Why, I'd be honored and delighted to write you people a letter," she said. Her skirt billowed around her.

"Thank you so much," said my mother. "But it's too much trouble for you, and also my husband is . . ."

"Oh, it's no trouble at all, no trouble at all. I tell you." She leaned forward, so that her chest freckles showed. "I know just how it is. It's a secret of course, but, you know, my natural father was Jewish. Can you see it? Just look at my skin."

"My husband," said my mother.

"I'd be honored and delighted," said Mrs. Lardner, with a little wave of her hands. "Just honored and delighted."

Mona was triumphant. "See, Mom," she said, waltzing around the kitchen when Mrs. Lardner left. "What did I

---

[17] Mandarin—official standard spoken language of China, based on the dialect spoken in the capital of Beijing.

tell you? 'I'm honored and delighted, just honored and delighted.'" She waved her hands in the air.

"You know, the Chinese have a saying," said my mother. "To do nothing is better than to overdo. You mean well, but you tell me now what will happen."

"I'll talk Dad into it," said Mona, still waltzing. "Or I bet Callie can. He'll do anything Callie says!"

"I can try, anyway," I said.

"Did you hear what I said?" said my mother. Mona bumped into the broom closet door. "You're not going to talk anything. You've already made enough trouble." She started on the dishes with a clatter.

Mona poked **diffidently**[18] at a mop.

I sponged off the counter. "Anyway," I ventured. "I bet our name'll never even come up."

"That's if we're lucky," said my mother.

"There's all these people waiting," I said.

"Good." She started on a pot.

I looked over at Mona, who was still **cowering**[19] in the broom closet. "In fact, there's some black family's been waiting so long, they're going to sue," I said.

My mother turned off the water. "Where'd you hear that?"

"Patty told me."

She turned the water back on, started to wash a dish, then put it down and shut the faucet.

"I'm sorry," said Mona.

"Forget it" said my mother. "Just forget it."

Booker turned out to be a model worker, whose boundless gratitude translated into a willingness to do anything. As he also learned quickly, he soon knew not only how to bus but how to cook, and how to wait tables, and how to keep the books. He fixed the walk-in door so that it stayed shut, reupholstered the torn seats in the dining room, and devised a system for tracking

---

[18] **diffidently**—timidly.

[19] **cowering**—crouching in fear.

inventory. The only stone in the rice was that he tended to be sickly; but, reliable even in illness, he would always send a friend to take his place. In this way, we got to know Ronald, Lynn, Dirk, and Cedric, all of whom, like Booker, had problems with their legal status, and were anxious to please. They weren't all as capable as Booker, though, with the exception of Cedric, whom my father often hired even when Booker was well. A round wag of a man who called Mona and me *shou hou*—skinny monkeys—he was a professed nonsmoker who was nevertheless always begging drags off other people's cigarettes. This last habit drove our head cook, Fernando, crazy, especially since, when refused a hit, Cedric would occasionally snitch one. Winking impishly at Mona and me, he would steal up to an ashtray, take a quick puff, and then break out laughing, so that the smoke came rolling out of his mouth in a great **incriminatory**[20] cloud. Fernando accused him of stealing fresh cigarettes, too, even whole packs.

"Why else do you think he's weaseling around in the back of the store all the time?" he said. His face was blotchy with anger. "The man is a thief."

Other members of the staff supported him in this **contention**,[21] and joined in on an "Operation Identification," which involved numbering and initialing their cigarettes—even though what they seemed to fear for wasn't so much their cigarettes as their jobs. Then one of the cooks quit; and, rather than promote someone, my father hired Cedric for the position. Rumor had it that Cedric was taking only half the normal salary; that Alex had been pressured to resign; and that my father was looking for a position with which to **placate**[22] Booker, who had been bypassed because of his health.

---

[20] **incriminatory**—guilt-proving.

[21] **contention**—claim; assertion.

[22] **placate**—reduce the anger of; appease.

The result was that Fernando categorically refused to work with Cedric.

"The only way I'll cook with that piece of slime," he said, shaking his huge, tattooed fist, "is if it's his ass frying on the grill."

My father **cajoled**[23] and cajoled, but in the end was simply forced to put them on different schedules.

The next week, Fernando got caught stealing a carton of minute steaks. My father would not tell even Mona and me how he knew to be standing by the back door when Fernando was on his way out, but everyone suspected Booker. Everyone but Fernando, that is, who was sure Cedric had been the tip-off. My father held a staff meeting, in which he tried to reassure everyone that Alex had left on his own, and that he had no intention of firing anyone. But though he was careful not to mention Fernando, everyone was so amazed that he was being allowed to stay that Fernando was incensed nonetheless.

"Don't you all be putting your bug eyes on me," he said. "He's the crook." He grabbed Cedric by the collar.

Cedric raised an eyebrow. "Cook, you mean," he said.

At this, Fernando punched Cedric in the mouth; and, the words he had just uttered notwithstanding, my father fired Fernando on the spot.

With everything that was happening, Mona and I were ready to be finishing up at the restaurant. It was almost time: The days were still stuffy with summer, but our window shade had started flapping in the evening as if gearing up to go out. That year, the breezes were full of salt, as they sometimes were when they came in from the east, and they blew anchors and docks through my mind like so many tumbleweeds, filling my dreams with wherries[24] and lobsters and grainy-faced men who squinted, day in and day out, at the sky.

---

[23] **cajoled**—coaxed; sweet-talked.
[24] wherries—light boats.

It was time for a change—you could feel it—and yet the pancake house was the same as ever. The day before school started, my father came home with bad news.

"Fernando called police," he said, wiping his hand on his pant leg.

My mother naturally wanted to know what police; and so, with much coughing and hawing, the long story began, the latest installment of which had the police calling Immigration, and Immigration sending an investigator. My mother sat stiff as whalebone as my father described how the man had summarily refused lunch on the house, and how my father had admitted, under pressure, that he knew there were "things" about his workers.

"So now what happens?"

My father didn't know. "Booker and Cedric went with him to the jail," he said. "But me, here I am." He laughed uncomfortably.

The next day, my father posted bail for "his boys," and waited **apprehensively**[25] for something to happen. The day after that, he waited again, and the day after that, he called our neighbor's law student son, who suggested my father call the Immigration Department under an **alias**.[26] My father took his advice; and it was thus that he discovered that Booker was right. It was illegal for aliens to work, but it wasn't to hire them.

In the happy interval that ensued, my father apologized to my mother, who in turn confessed about the country club, for which my father had no choice but to forgive her. Then he turned his attention back to "his boys."

My mother didn't see that there was anything to do.

"I like to talking to the judge," said my father.

"This is not China," said my mother.

"I'm only talking to him. I'm not give him money unless he wants it."

---

[25] **apprehensively**—with anxiety about the future; fearfully.

[26] **alias**—assumed name.

Los Gatos High School

"You're going to land up in jail."

"So what else I should do?" My father threw up his hands. "Those are my boys."

"Your boys!" exploded my mother. "What about your family? What about your wife?"

My father took a long sip of tea. "You know," he said finally, "in the war my father sent our cook to the soldiers to use. He always said it—the province comes before the town, the town comes before the family."

"A restaurant is not a town," said my mother.

My father sipped at his tea again. "You know, when I first come to the United States, I also had to hide-and-seek with those deportation guys. If people did not helping me, I am not here today."

My mother **scrutinized**[27] her hem.

After a minute, I volunteered that before seeing a judge, he might try a lawyer.

He turned. "Since when did you become so afraid like your mother?"

I started to say that it wasn't a matter of fear, but he cut me off.

"What I need today," he said, "is a son."

My father and I spent the better part of the next day standing on lines at the Immigration office. He did not get to speak to a judge, but with much persistence he managed to speak to a special clerk, who tried to persuade him that it was not her place to extend him advice. My father, though, shamelessly **plied**[28] her with compliments and offers of free pancakes, until she finally conceded that she personally doubted anything would happen to either Cedric or Booker.

"Especially if they're 'needed workers,'" she said, rubbing at the red marks her glasses left on her nose. She yawned. "Have you thought about sponsoring them to become permanent residents?"

---

[27] **scrutinized**—carefully studied; examined closely.

[28] **plied**—continued supplying.

Could he do that? My father was overjoyed. And what if he saw to it right away? Would she perhaps put in a good word with the judge?

She yawned again, her nostrils flaring. "Don't worry," she said. "They'll get a fair hearing."

My father returned **jubilant.**[29] Booker and Cedric hailed him as their savior. He was like a father to them, they said; and, laughing and clapping, they made him tell the story over and over, sorting through the details like jewels. And how old was the assistant judge? And what did she say?

That evening, my father tipped the paperboy a dollar and bought a pot of mums for my mother, who **suffered**[30] them to be placed on the dining room table. The next night, he took us all out to dinner. Then on Saturday, Mona found a letter and some money in an envelope on my father's chair at the restaurant.

Dear Mr. Chang,
You are the grat boss. But, we do not like to trial, so will runing away now. Plese to excus us. People saying the law in America is fears like dragon. Here is only $140. We hope some day we can pay back the rest bale. You will getting intrest, as you diserving, so grat a boss you are. Thank you for every thing. In next life you will be burn in rich family, with no more pancaks.
Yours truley,
Booker + Cedric

In the weeks that followed, my father went to the pancake house for crises, but otherwise hung around our house, fiddling idly with the sump pump and boiler in an effort, he said, to get ready for winter. It was as though he had gone into retirement, except that instead

---

[29] **jubilant**—triumphantly joyful.

[30] **suffered**—permitted.

of moving south, he had moved to the basement. He even took to showering my mother with little attentions, and to calling her "old girl," and when we finally heard that the club had entertained all the applications it could for the year, he was so sympathetic that he seemed more disappointed than my mother.

QUESTIONS TO CONSIDER

1. Why do you think the father doesn't talk about his grandfather and life back in China until he has established his own successful business?

2. How do the mother and father differ in their ideas about being a part of American society?

3. Why does the father consider Booker and Cedric "his boys"?

4. How does the father explain the relative importance of his wife, his family, and the restaurant? How does his sense of priorities affect the decisions he makes?

A Chronology
of Asian-American
History

BY JUDY YUNG

Judy Yung is a librarian, historian, writer, and professor with a special interest in Chinese-American history. She authored Chinese Women of America: A Pictorial History *and coauthored* Island: Poetry and History of Chinese Immigrants on Angel Island, 1910–1940. *The following selection, "A Chronology of Asian American History," was taken from the Appendix of* Making Waves: An Anthology of Writing by and About Asian American Women *(1989), edited by Asian Women United of California.*

1785

Three Chinese seamen land in Baltimore.

1790

First known native of India reported in Salem, Massachusetts.

1790

Naturalization Act of 1790 grants to all "free white persons" the right to U.S. citizenship.

1834

Afong Moy, the first known Chinese woman in the United States, put on display in a New York theater.

1843

First known Japanese immigrant arrives in the United States.

1848

First Chinese immigrants—two men and one woman—arrive in San Francisco on the American brig, *Eagle*.

1848–1853

Gold Rush in California. By 1852, 20,000 Chinese arrive to join in the Gold Rush. Foreign Miners' Tax imposed in 1850 against the Chinese.

1852

180 Chinese indentured laborers[1] brought to Hawaii to work in the sugar plantations.

1854

In *People* v. *Hall*, the California Supreme Court rules testimony by Chinese, blacks, **mulattos**,[2] and Native Americans against whites invalid; later repealed in 1872.

---

[1] indentured laborers—workers bound by contract to work for a person or company for a period of time in return for their travel and other expenses.

[2] **mulattos**—persons of mixed white and black racial heritage.

1866–1869

Construction of the first transcontinental railroad with largely Chinese labor. Some 2,000 Chinese workers strike for improved working conditions.

1868

148 (141 men, 6 women, and 1 child) Japanese contracted laborers brought to Hawaii to work in the sugar plantations.

1870–1885

The Anti-Chinese Movement. The Chinese, singled out as scapegoats during a time of labor unrest, become targets of discriminatory laws and racial violence.

1880

California Civil Code amended to prohibit the issuance of a marriage license to a white person and a "Negro, Mulatto, or Mongolian"; Filipinos added in 1933; [Code] repealed in 1948.

1882

The Chinese Exclusion Act bans immigration of Chinese laborers to the United States and prohibits Chinese from becoming naturalized citizens; repealed in 1943.

1882

United States negotiates first trade treaty with Korea and approximately 100 students and diplomats from Korea enter the country for training.

1885

The Meiji government officially sanctions the emigration of 30,000 Japanese to Hawaii as contract laborers between 1885 and 1894.

1889

First two Korean women arrive in the United States— Mrs. Lee Wan-yong and Mrs. Lee Chae-yon, both wives of Korean diplomats.

1898

The Spanish-American War ends with the signing of the Treaty of Paris, giving Cuba, Puerto Rico, and the Philippines to the United States. Filipinos declared "wards" and need no visas to travel to the United States. Filipino wives of Spanish-American War veterans allowed to come as war brides.

1898

United States annexes Hawaii.

1903

93 Korean contract laborers arrive in Hawaii to work in the sugar plantations. Approximately, 7,000 Koreans (including 637 women) immigrate to Hawaii between 1903 and 1905, when Japan establishes a protectorate over Korea and formally ends emigration.

1903

Pensionado Act allows Filipino students to come to the United States for education.

1904–1924

6,000 to 15,000 South Asians, the majority of whom are male farmers originally from the Punjab province of India, immigrate to the Pacific coast of Canada and the United States.

1905

The Asiatic Exclusion League organizes in San Francisco to prevent the immigration of Asians.

1907

White lumber mill workers drive East Indian workers out of Bellingham, Washington.

1907–1908

Gentlemen's Agreement between United States and Japan. Japan imposes limitations on emigration of Japanese and Korean laborers to the United States and rights of Japanese insured in America. Wives, including picture brides,[3] and family members are exempted.

1907

210 Filipinos (188 men, 20 women, and 2 children) arrive in Hawaii to work in the sugar plantations. From 1907 to 1924, 46,605 men and 7,187 women immigrate to Hawaii.

1910

One woman and two girls arrive in San Francisco from India, bringing the total number of Indian women on the West Coast to six.

1913

The California Alien Land Act, aimed at Japanese farmers, bars aliens from owning land; further restrictions are added in 1921 and 1923; repealed in 1948.

1916

Kanta Gupta becomes the first Indian woman to apply for U.S. citizenship.

1917

The 1917 Immigration Act establishes "barred zones" to prohibit immigration of laborers from virtually all of Asia except for Japan.

1918

Act of 9 May 1918, extends the right of naturalization, regardless of race, to one who enlisted and served in the U.S. armed forces.

1922

Ozawa v. *United States* interprets Japanese aliens as ineligible for U.S. citizenship through naturalization.

---

[3] picture brides—name given to Asian women whose marriages were arranged in their native country by the parents of the couple. The woman's picture was sent to the groom so he could recognize his prospective bride when she arrived in the United States.

1922

The Cable Act provides that woman citizens will lose their U.S. citizenship if they marry aliens ineligible for citizenship; unlike white women, Asian American women cannot regain their U.S. citizenship through naturalization; repealed in 1931.

1923

United States v. *Thind* rules aliens from India ineligible for American citizenship.

1924

Immigration Quota Act excludes all aliens ineligible for citizenship (all Asians except Hawaiians and Filipinos) and allows entry of alien wives of Chinese merchants, but not alien wives of U.S. citizens until 1930, when Public Law 349 admits wives married before 26 May 1924.

1929

Race riots break out around Watsonville, California, against Filipino agricultural laborers.

1931

Filipinos who served in the U.S. armed forces now eligible for U.S. citizenship.

1934

Morrison v. *California* holds Filipinos ineligible for citizenship.

1934

Tydings-McDuffie Act promises independence to the Philippines in ten years and assigns an annual quota of fifty Filipino immigrants.

1935

Public Law 162 authorizes naturalization of certain resident alien World War I veterans, despite not being white or of African descent.

1942

Executive Order 9066 authorizes the military to prescribe military zones from which persons may be excluded; 112,000 Japanese Americans are incarcerated in ten relocation centers as a result.

1943

Congress repeals Chinese exclusion acts, removes racial bar to naturalization of Chinese aliens, and establishes annual quota of 105 for Chinese immigration to the United States.

1945

War Brides Act, GI Fiancées Act, and Act of 9 August 1946 facilitate entrance of Asian war brides, fiancées, and children. An estimated 200,000 Asian war brides immigrate to the United States after World War II.

1946

United States declares the Philippines independent, sets annual immigration quota of 100 for Filipinos and Asian Indians, and grants them the right of naturalization.

1946

Philippine Trade Act grants nonquota immigrant status to Philippine citizens, their spouses, and children who have resided in the United States for a continuous period of three years prior to 30 November 1941.

1950

Act of 19 August 1950 gives spouses and minor children of members of the American armed forces nonquota immigration status if married before 19 March 1952, aiding primarily aliens of Japanese and Korean ancestry. As a result, between 1950 and 1965, 6,423 war brides arrive in the United States.

1952

The McCarran-Walter Act upholds the national-origin quota based on the 1920 U.S. Census but retains the same quotas for Asia-Pacific triangle countries of the 1924 Immigration Act; aliens previously ineligible for citizenship are allowed naturalization rights.

1965

The Immigration and Naturalization Act of 1965 abolishes the national-origin quotas and substitutes hemispheric quotas; eastern hemisphere quota set at 170,000, with a limit of 20,000 per country.

1965

Voting Rights Act guarantees all citizens equal access to electoral politics.

1967

The U.S. Supreme Court rules that states cannot outlaw intermarriages by race.

1971

Sub-Title II of the McCarran Act, which provides for detention camps, repealed by Congress.

1976

President Gerald Ford **rescinds**[4] Executive Order 9066, which authorized the relocation of Japanese Americans from the Pacific coast.

1976–1985

762,100 Southeast Asian refugees, including many who fled by boat, are resettled in the United States.

1980

Commission on Wartime Relocation and Internment of Civilians formed to investigate the justification for the

---

[4] **rescinds**—takes back; voids; repeals.

internment of Japanese Americans during World War II. Later findings conclude there was no military necessity for internment.

1982

President Ronald Reagan establishes a 1982 ceiling of 10,000 Southeast Asian admissions.

1982

Congress passes Public Law 97–359 (American Immigration Act), offering top priority for immigration to children in Korea, Vietnam, Laos, Cambodia, or Thailand known to have been fathered by a U.S. citizen.

1983

National Committee for Japanese American Redress files federal lawsuit on behalf of an estimated 120,000 internees, asking for **monetary redress.**[5]

1988

Congress passes bill publicly apologizing for the internment of Japanese Americans during World War II and paying $20,000 to each eligible former internee.

---

[5] **monetary redress**—compensation in the form of money.

QUESTIONS TO CONSIDER

1. Where and for what purposes were Asian Americans encouraged or permitted to come to the United States?

2. What groups of people seemed to be naturalized more easily than others? What, in your opinion, is the reason that these groups were favored?

3. Why do you think so many immigration-related laws were passed only to be repealed or changed by passage of a new law later on? What conclusions can you draw from this pattern?

4. What specific changes in policy and laws focused on women? Why do you think these changes were made?

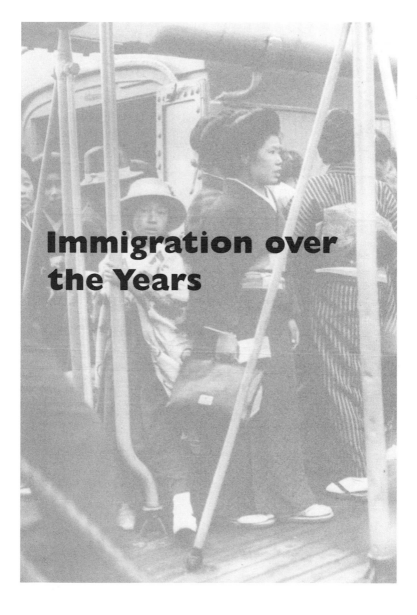

Immigration over the Years

▲
A sketch from 1881 shows the tight quarters Chinese immigrants endured on the long journey to the United States.

◀ Japanese immigrants aboard the liner *Shinyu Maru* arrive in San Francisco, California, on July 25, 1920.

▲

New Citizens Asian immigrants earn their naturalization certificates at a citizenship ceremony in San Francisco, California.

Vietnam War Mobs of South Vietnamese try to scale the wall of the United States Embassy in Saigon on April 29, 1975, hoping to reach the last evacuation helicopters leaving for America. A day later, a defeated South Vietnam surrendered to North Vietnam. ▶

▲

Illegal Entry A Coast Guard boarding team approaches the cargo ship *Xing Da* 600 miles off the New England coast on October 2, 1996. Three men from New York were later indicted on charges of attempting to smuggle more than 100 illegal aliens from Asia into the United States by hiding them in the ship's cargo hold.

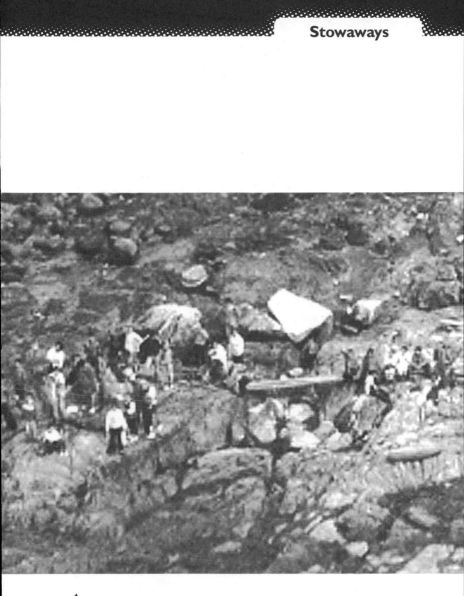

▲

A group of stowaways wanders the shore of the Queen Charlotte Islands in the Canadian province of British Columbia on August 11, 1999. They have abandoned ship in order to avoid the Canadian authorities.

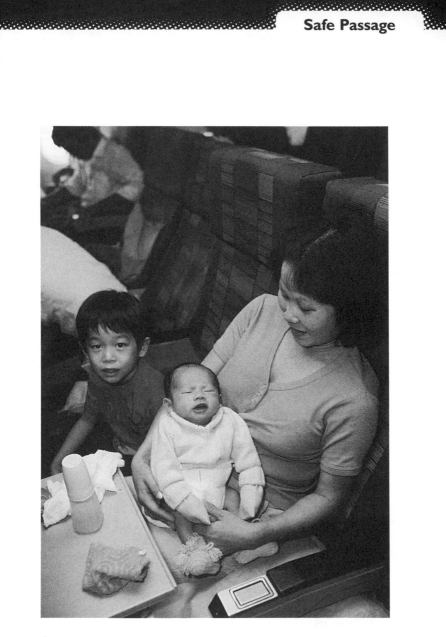

▲

A Vietnamese mother and her children travel by plane to Seattle, Washington, where they will begin their new life.

Enduring Hardships

Claremont and Colusa

BY MARY PAIK LEE

Mary Paik Lee (1900–1995) was born in Pyongyang, Korea, and moved with her parents to Hawaii in 1905. Two years later the growing family moved to southern California and from there to northern California. In this excerpt from her autobiography, Quiet Odyssey: A Pioneer Korean Woman in America *(1990), Lee describes the family's struggles in California. The story takes place around 1910, a few years after the Gentlemen's Agreement between the United States and Japan posed limitations on the immigration of Japanese and Korean laborers to the United States. This account is a treasure, for it documents the experiences of one of the few Korean children living on the West Coast at that time.*

We lived in Riverside for four or five years, but father became concerned about Mother's health—the work of cooking for thirty men was too much for her. She was a small woman, only four feet eleven inches tall, and she was expecting another baby. So we paid off the

Chinese merchants who had helped us get started, paid all our debts to friends, and moved to Claremont, not too far away. It was a quiet college town with many school buildings. We moved into a duplex building, where an old friend, Martha Kim, was living with her parents. It was across the street from the railroad station and a huge citrus-packing house. Those were the days before frozen fruit juices, so after the choice fruit was packed, the **culls**[1] were piled up in boxes in back of the buildings to be taken to the dump once a week. Because of this, we were fortunate that we could enjoy all the discarded fruit.

Our move to Claremont turned out to be our first experience with the American way of living. The new house seemed huge after our little shack. It had several rooms with beds, chairs, and other furniture. The kitchen had a gas stove, electric lights, and a sink with faucets for cold and hot water. But all that was as nothing compared with what we found in the bathroom. There was a big white tub with faucets at one end—I couldn't believe it was the place for taking our baths. And the biggest surprise of all was the toilet. Father flushed it to show us how it operated. He must have seen these wonders before somewhere, because he wasn't surprised at anything. For the first time, I felt glad that we had come to America.

Father found a job as a janitor in the nearby apartment buildings. He told Meung[2] and me to ask the **tenants**[3] if we could do their laundry, and also to ask our schoolteachers the same thing. On foot, Meung had to pick up the dirty laundry in a big basket and return it later. I helped with the laundry before and after school and with the ironing at night. In Claremont we had our first experience with an electric iron. Before this we had heated

---

[1] **culls**—(fruit) rejected because of its inferior quality.

[2] Meung—the narrator's brother.

[3] **tenants**—people who live in the building; renters.

the old "sad irons,"[4] as they were called in those days, on the wood stove. It was such a relief to use the electric iron. No more going back and forth to the wood stove for a hot iron. No more kerosene lamps, hunting for firewood, and outhouses. Life was getting better. Every Saturday Father bought a beef roast, and every Sunday we had pot roast with mashed potatoes and bread. This was our introduction to American food, and it tasted wonderful. A small group of Koreans lived in Claremont. They came together to worship on Sundays in an old building. There was no minister, so Father preached there several times. Arthur was born in Claremont on December 2, 1910. The memory of our short stay there is a pleasant one.

Unfortunately Father's wages were so low in Claremont that it was difficult to make a living. So, a year later, we moved to Colusa in northern California, hoping to find work there. It turned out we had made a disastrous move. Father could not find any kind of work. There was a depression in 1911, and the situation was so bad the Salvation Army offered a bowl of soup and a piece of bread to each hungry person in town. But when I asked if we could go and get some, Father said no. He didn't want us to be **humiliated**[5] by asking for help.

The feeling towards Orientals in southern California had not been friendly, but we had been tolerated. In the northern part of the state, we found the situation to be much worse. Although we found a house on the outskirts of town, the townspeople's attitude towards us was chilling. Father told Meung and me to ask our school-teachers for their laundry. Once again, Meung had to fetch and deliver, carrying a basket on foot. Since we lived on the outskirts of town, it was a hard job for him, but he never complained. But because of the negative

---

[4] "sad irons"—flatirons with two pointed ends. *Sad*, a dialect word, means "heavy."

[5] **humiliated**—lowered in pride, dignity, or respect; embarrassed; ashamed.

feeling towards Orientals in Colusa, we never got enough clothes to launder, and we could not earn enough money to meet our needs.

After paying the rent, light, water, and other bills, we had very little left over for food. Mother would tell me to buy a five-pound sack of flour, a small can of baking powder, salt, and two cans of Carnation milk for the baby. The two cans of milk had to last for one week: it was **diluted**[6] with so much water, it didn't look like anything nourishing. Mother made tiny biscuits each morning and served one biscuit and a tin cup of water to each of us three times a day. During the time we lived in Colusa, we had no rice, meat, or anything besides biscuits to eat. Nonetheless, when we sat down to eat, Father would pray, thanking God for all our blessings. This used to irritate me. At the age of eleven years, I couldn't think of anything to be thankful for. Once he was sitting out on the porch smoking after dinner, and I asked him what we had to be so thankful for. He said, "Don't you remember why we came here?" I had forgotten that the fate of our family in Korea was much worse than ours. Nevertheless, my stomach ached for lack of food, and I had severe cramps. One evening the pain was so bad I got up to fill myself with water, which helped somewhat. As I neared the kitchen, I saw Father and Mother sitting across from each other at the table holding hands, with tears flowing down their faces. I realized then how much agony they were suffering, and that my own feelings were as nothing compared with theirs. I had been so **absorbed**[7] in myself that the thought of my parents' suffering had never entered my mind. Seeing them that way made me realize how ignorant I was. It awakened me to the realities of life.

---

[6] **diluted**—thinned (in order to make the milk go further as a way of saving money).

[7] **absorbed**—exclusively occupied; engrossed.

I thought maybe I could get work cleaning some-one's home to help out. Since my schoolteacher was the only one I could talk to, I asked her if she knew where I could get housework. She said that the principal lived in a big house, that his wife might need someone to help her. So I went to the principal and asked if his wife needed someone to do the cleaning in his home. He said that he would find out and let me know.

The next day I went to his office and found out that his wife was willing to try me. She said I should work before and after school, and all day Saturdays and Sundays. The wages were to be one dollar a week. In my ignorance, that sounded good to me. I asked where he lived and walked past it on my way home. It was a big, beautiful house, quite far from ours, with a large lawn in front and colorful flowers all around. When I told Father about it, he shook his head and didn't say a word. As if he didn't know it, I said that one dollar would buy twenty loaves of bread, and that it would help feed the younger children who were hungry. Bread cost five cents a loaf then. He said it was too much work for me, but I could try it. Father left the room and went outside to smoke his pipe. Many years later, he told me he had felt humiliated to hear his eleven-year-old daughter tell him that her one-dollar-a-week wages were needed to feed the family. I was too young and ignorant to know how my words had hurt him.

I was totally ignorant of what my employers expected of me, but I was stubborn enough to make the attempt. My secret reason for wanting this job was that I was hoping to get something more than a tiny biscuit and water to eat, but my punishment came in an unexpected way. Before I left home in the morning, Father gave me advice about how I was to behave in my first American home. He showed me how to set a table with napkins, and so forth. He said I should eat in the kitchen, never with the family. I left home at 6 A.M., reached the principal's house before 7 A.M., and was surprised to see his wife. She looked like the pictures of the fat lady in the circus—a huge woman. I also met her son, who was about twenty years old. I helped the woman prepare breakfast and I set the table. Before they sat down to eat, she gave me a cup of black coffee with no sugar, milk, or cream, and she took the trouble to slice a piece of bread so thin that, when I held it up to the light of the window, I could see the outline of the tree outside. That was about the same amount of food I would have had at home. I had to laugh at myself.

After the family finished eating, I cleared the table, washed the dishes, and cleaned up in the kitchen. Then I had to walk to school while the principal drove in his car. His son had a car also. Very few people in town owned cars, so two cars in one home was certainly unusual. When I told Father about it, he said that it *was* surprising, considering the low salaries of teachers. About fifteen years later, as I was passing a newsstand, I saw the principal's name in the headline of a paper. I stopped to read it. The article stated that Mr. So-and-So had been arrested for **embezzling**[8] school funds. This had apparently been going on for years. No wonder he had a big, beautiful home and two cars in the family.

After school I went back to the principal's house, helped his wife prepare dinner, and set the table. Then I cleaned the other rooms while dinner was being prepared. She gave me a piece of bread and a few spoons of this and that for my meal. When I cleared the table, she put all the leftovers in dishes, covered them tightly, and put them in the ice box.[9] I guess she was afraid I would eat their food. After washing the dishes and cleaning up the kitchen, I was told I could leave.

---

[8] **embezzling**—stealing.

[9] ice box—insulated box with shelves. Blocks of ice sitting on the bottom preserved food kept on shelves above; ice boxes preceded electric refrigerators.

On Saturdays, I had to wash all the sheets, pillow-cases, towels, and clothes in a big washtub, scrubbing them on a washboard in the backyard, rinsing them, hanging them on a line to dry, and taking them into the house after they were dry. There were no washing machines in those days. Everything had to be done by hand. On Sunday mornings, I sprinkled all the clothes that needed ironing and ironed all day. By nightfall, I was so tired I could hardly walk home. I had to admit to myself that the work was too much for me. Finally, summer vacation came. Father said that he was going to Dinuba, near Fresno, to work in the fruit orchards there to try to make some money. Thus, I should stay home and help Mother while he was away. I was really glad to have an excuse to quit my job. After that, I learned to listen to my elders and not to be such a stubborn fool over things I knew nothing about.

One day we heard music outside the house. Looking out the window, we saw a small truck painted in bright colors with a big picture of an ice cream cone filled with white ice cream. All my younger brothers had their faces pressed against the window, wondering what the truck was. We had never tasted ice cream. Seeing so many children, the man thought that surely someone would come out to buy from him. After waiting several minutes, he gave up and left. The children looked around at Father with questions in their eyes, not daring to say a word. That must have been an agonizing moment for my parents. I looked at their sad, desperate faces and felt sorry for them. Father asked all of us to come into the kitchen and sit down at the table. He took out all the money he had and said that we were not earning enough money to buy everything we wanted, and that we had to pay for several things before we could even buy food to eat. Picking up a few coins, he said, "We have to save this much every week in order to pay the rent for this house, otherwise the owner will not let us live here.

Then we have to pay so much for the electric lights, gas for the stove, water, and laundering supplies. That is why we cannot buy enough food to eat three times a day. There is nothing left for such things as ice cream cones." It was a lesson in economics that even a five-year-old child could understand. There were five children in the family then, and ice cream cones cost five cents apiece. Twenty-five cents was a lot of money when one did not have it. From then on, the children never looked out the window when the music sounded, and the ice cream man never stopped at our house. The children never asked for anything after that.

When Father left for Dinuba, Mother, Meung, and I tried to keep going as usual, but we could not do any better. We still had just one biscuit with a cup of water three times a day. Father came back from Dinuba in September, looking so sick and tired it was pitiful. We were shocked at his appearance and wished he had not left home. After paying for his room, board, and the train fare home, there was little left over, but he said he had just enough for us to move out of Colusa.

QUESTIONS TO CONSIDER

1. In what ways was the move to Claremont an improvement in the family's situation?

2. What made life so much more difficult once the family moved to Colusa?

3. What does Mary Paik Lee learn about her family and the hardships of life in general from her experiences in Colusa?

4. How would you describe Mary's personal qualities? In what ways does she seem like a typical eleven-year-old? In what ways is she unusual for a girl her age?

5. What was the economic climate at the time of this story? How, in your opinion, might it have affected the way immigrants were treated?

from

Farewell to Manzanar

BY JEANNE WAKATSUKI HOUSTON
AND JAMES D. HOUSTON

Jeanne Wakatsuki Houston was born in the United States in 1934. She was seven years old when she and her family were uprooted from their home in Long Beach, California, because of the Japanese bombing of the naval base in Pearl Harbor that brought the United States into World War II. Her father, a fisherman, was considered an enemy alien and was separated from his family for a year. The rest of the family were among the first people sent to Manzanar Internment Camp near Owens Valley, California, and they were among the last to leave. In this excerpt from Farewell to Manzanar (1973), a memoir of her World War II experiences, Houston describes her life shortly before the bombing of Pearl Harbor and the challenges she and her family faced after the United States entered the war.

"What Is Pearl Harbor?"

On that first weekend in December there must have been twenty or twenty-five boats getting ready to leave. I had just turned seven. I remember it was Sunday because I was out of school, which meant I could go down to the wharf and watch. In those days—1941—there was no smog around Long Beach.[1] The water was clean, the sky a sharp Sunday blue, with all the engines of that white sardine fleet[2] puttering up into it, and a lot of yelling, especially around Papa's boat. Papa loved to give orders. He had attended military school in Japan until the age of seventeen, and part of him never got over that. My oldest brothers, Bill and Woody, were his crew. They would have to check the nets again, and check the fuel tanks again, and run back to the grocery store for some more cigarettes, and then somehow everything had been done, and they were easing away from the wharf, joining the line of boats heading out past the lighthouse, into the harbor.

Papa's boat was called *The Nereid*—long, white, low-slung, with a foredeck wheel cabin.[3] He had another smaller boat, called *The Waka* (a short version of our name), which he kept in Santa Monica, where we lived. But *The Nereid* was his pride. It was worth about $25,000 before the war, and the way he stood in the cabin steering toward open water you would think the whole fleet was under his command. Papa had a mustache then. He wore knee-high rubber boots, a rust-colored turtleneck Mama had knitted him, and a black skipper's hat. He liked to hear himself called "Skipper."

Through one of the big canneries he had made a deal to pay for *The Nereid* with percentages of each catch, and he was anxious to get it paid off. He didn't much like working for someone else if he could help it. A lot of fishermen around San Pedro Harbor had similar contracts with the canneries. In typical Japanese fashion, they all wanted to be independent commercial fishermen, yet

---

[1] Long Beach—a city on the coast of southern California. The Port of Long Beach and the Port of Los Angeles form a major harbor.

[2] sardine fleet—group of small ships that fish for sardines.

[3] foredeck wheel cabin—enclosed, windowed structure located at the front (or bow) of a boat and containing the steering mechanism.

they almost always fished together. They would take off from Terminal Island,[4] help each other find the schools of sardine, share nets and radio equipment—competing and cooperating at the same time.

You never knew how long they'd be gone, a couple of days, sometimes a week, sometimes a month, depending on the fish. From the wharf we waved good-bye— my mother, Bill's wife, Woody's wife Chizu, and me. We yelled at them to have a good trip, and after they were out of earshot and the sea had swallowed their engine noises, we kept waving. Then we just stood there with the other women, watching. It was a kind of duty, perhaps a way of adding a little good luck to the voyage, or warding off the bad. It was also marvelously warm, almost summery, the way December days can be sometimes in southern California. When the boats came back, the women who lived on Terminal Island would be rushing to the canneries. But for the moment there wasn't much else to do. We watched until the boats became a row of tiny white gulls on the horizon. Our **vigil**[5] would end when they slipped over the edge and disappeared. You had to squint against the glare to keep them sighted, and with every blink you expected the last white speck to be gone.

But this time they didn't disappear. They kept floating out there, suspended, as if the horizon had finally become what it always seemed to be from shore: the sea's limit, beyond which no man could sail. They floated awhile, then they began to grow, tiny gulls becoming boats again, a white **armada**[6] cruising toward us.

"They're coming back," my mother said.

"Why would they be coming back?" Chizu said.

---

[4] Terminal Island—a large island located in the Port of Los Angeles between the cities of San Pedro and Long Beach.

[5] **vigil**—watch; surveillance.

[6] **armada**—fleet of ships, usually warships.

"Something with the engine."

"Maybe somebody got hurt."

"But they wouldn't *all* come back," Mama said, bewildered.

Another woman said, "Maybe there's a storm coming."

They all glanced at the sky, scanning the **unmarred**[7] horizon. Mama shook her head. There was no explanation. No one had ever seen anything like this before. We watched and waited, and when the boats were still about half a mile off the lighthouse, a fellow from the cannery came running down to the wharf shouting that the Japanese had just bombed Pearl Harbor.

Chizu said to Mama, "What does he mean? What is Pearl Harbor?"

Mama yelled at him, "What is Pearl Harbor?"

But he was running along the docks, like Paul Revere,[8] bringing the news, and didn't have time to explain.

That night Papa burned the flag he had brought with him from Hiroshima[9] thirty-five years earlier. It was such a beautiful piece of material, I couldn't believe he was doing that. He burned a lot of papers too, documents, anything that might suggest he still had some connection with Japan. These precautions didn't do him much good. He was not only an **alien;**[10] he held a commercial fishing license, and in the early days of the war the FBI was picking up all such men, for fear they were somehow making contact with enemy ships off the coast. Papa himself knew it would only be a matter of time.

They got him two weeks later, when we were staying overnight at Woody's place, on Terminal Island. Five

---

[7] **unmarred**—unblemished; flawless; perfectly smooth.

[8] Paul Revere—hero of the American Revolution who, according to legend, rode through the countryside alerting the Minutemen that "the British are coming!"

[9] Hiroshima—a major city in Japan that later was the site of the first atomic bomb attack.

[10] **alien**—unnaturalized foreign resident; not a citizen.

hundred Japanese families lived there then, and FBI deputies had been questioning everyone, **ransacking**[11] houses for anything that could conceivably be used for signaling planes or ships or that indicated loyalty to the Emperor. Most of the houses had radios with a short-wave band and a high aerial on the roof so that wives could make contact with the fishing boats during these long cruises. To the FBI every radio owner was a potential **saboteur**.[12] The **confiscators**[13] were often deputies sworn in hastily during the turbulent days right after Pearl Harbor, and these men seemed to be acting out the general panic, seeing sinister possibilities in the most ordinary household items: flashlights, kitchen knives, cameras, lanterns, toy swords.

If Papa were trying to avoid arrest, he wouldn't have gone near that island. But I think he knew it was futile to hide out or resist. The next morning two FBI men in fedora hats[14] and trench coats—like out of a thirties movie—knocked on Woody's door, and when they left, Papa was between them. He didn't struggle. There was no point to it. He had become a man without a country. The land of his birth was at war with America; yet after thirty-five years here he was still prevented by law from becoming an American citizen. He was suddenly a man with no rights who looked exactly like the enemy.

About all he had left at this point was his tremendous dignity. He was tall for a Japanese man, nearly six feet, lean and hard and healthy-skinned from the sea. He was over fifty. Ten children and a lot of hard luck had worn him down, had worn away most of the **arrogance**[15] he came to this country with. But he still had dignity,

---

[11] **ransacking**—vigorously searching.

[12] **saboteur**—enemy agent who would hinder or undermine the war effort.

[13] **confiscators**—people who have the authority to seize property.

[14] fedora hats—hats made of soft felt. The brim of a fedora can be turned up or down and the crown creased lengthwise.

[15] **arrogance**—prideful sense of one's own importance.

and he would not let those deputies push him out the door. He led them.

Mama knew they were taking all the alien men first to an interrogation center right there on the island. Some were simply being questioned and released. In the beginning she wasn't too worried; at least she wouldn't let herself be. But it grew dark and he wasn't back. Another day went by and we still had heard nothing. Then word came that he had been taken into custody and shipped out. Where to, or for how long? No one knew. All my brothers' attempts to find out were fruitless.

What had they charged him with? We didn't know that either, until an article appeared the next day in the Santa Monica paper, saying he had been arrested for delivering oil to Japanese submarines offshore.

My mother began to weep. It seems now that she wept for days. She was a small, plump woman who laughed easily and cried easily, but I had never seen her cry like this. I couldn't understand it. I remember clinging to her legs, wondering why everyone was crying. This was the beginning of a terrible, frantic time for all my family. But I myself didn't cry about Papa, or have any **inkling**[16] of what was wrenching Mama's heart, until the next time I saw him, almost a year later.

Shikata Ga Nai

In December of 1941 Papa's disappearance didn't bother me nearly so much as the world I soon found myself in.

He had been a jack-of-all-trades. When I was born he was farming near Inglewood.[17] Later, when he started fishing, we moved to Ocean Park, near Santa Monica, and until they picked him up, that's where we lived, in a big frame house with a brick fireplace, a block back

---

[16] **inkling**—hint; vague notion.

[17] Inglewood—a suburb of Los Angeles, north of Long Beach.

from the beach. We were the only Japanese family in the neighborhood. Papa liked it that way. He didn't want to be labeled or grouped by anyone. But with him gone and no way of knowing what to expect, my mother moved all of us down to Terminal Island. Woody already lived there, and one of my older sisters had married a Terminal Island boy. Mama's first concern now was to keep the family together; and once the war began, she felt safer there than isolated racially in Ocean Park. But for me, at age seven, the island was a country as foreign as India or Arabia would have been. It was the first time I had lived among other Japanese, or gone to school with them, and I was terrified all the time.

This was partly Papa's fault. One of his threats to keep us younger kids in line was "I'm going to sell you to the Chinaman." When I had entered kindergarten two years earlier, I was the only Oriental in the class. They sat me next to a Caucasian girl who happened to have very slanted eyes. I looked at her and began to scream, certain Papa had sold me out at last. My fear of her ran so deep I could not speak of it, even to Mama, couldn't explain why I was screaming. For two weeks I had nightmares about this girl, until the teachers finally moved me to the other side of the room. And it was still with me, this fear of Oriental faces, when we moved to Terminal Island.

In those days it was a company town, a ghetto owned and controlled by the canneries. The men went after fish, and whenever the boats came back—day or night—the women would be called to process the catch while it was fresh. One in the afternoon or four in the morning, it made no difference. My mother had to go to work right after we moved there. I can still hear the whistle—two toots for French's, three for Van Camp's[18]—and she and Chizu would be out of bed in the middle of the night, heading for the cannery.

---

[18] French's and Van Camp's are two food companies.

The house we lived in was nothing more than a shack, a barracks with single plank walls and rough wooden floors, like the cheapest kind of migrant workers' housing. The people around us were hardworking, boisterous, a little proud of their nickname, *yo-go-re*, which meant literally *uncouth one*, or roughneck, or dead-end kid. They not only spoke Japanese exclusively, they spoke a dialect peculiar to Kyushu,[19] where their families had come from in Japan, a rough, fisherman's language, full of oaths and insults. Instead of saying *ba-ka-ta-re*, a common insult meaning *stupid*, Terminal Islanders would say *ba-ka-ya-ro*, a coarser and exclusively masculine use of the word, which implies gross stupidity. They would **swagger**[20] and pick on outsiders and persecute anyone who didn't speak as they did. That was what made my own time there so hateful. I had never spoken anything but English, and the other kids in the second grade despised me for it. They were tough and mean, like **ghetto**[21] kids anywhere. Each day after school I dreaded their ambush. My brother Kiyo, three years older, would wait for me at the door, where we would decide whether to run straight home together, or split up, or try a new and unexpected route.

None of these kids ever actually attacked. It was the threat that frightened us, their fearful looks, and the noises they would make, like miniature Samurai,[22] in a language we couldn't understand.

At the time it seemed we had been living under this reign of fear for years. In fact, we lived there about two months. Late in February the navy decided to clear Terminal Island completely. Even though most of us were American-born, it was dangerous having that

---

[19] Kyushu—the third largest and the most southern of Japan's four islands.

[20] **swagger**—act boastfully; threaten; brag.

[21] **ghetto**—from the section of a city where a minority group is forced to live, either by economic circumstances or by law.

[22] Samurai—Japanese warriors.

many Orientals so close to the Long Beach Naval Station, on the opposite end of the island. We had known something like this was coming. But, like Papa's arrest, not much could be done ahead of time. There were four of us kids still young enough to be living with Mama, plus Granny, her mother, sixty-five then, speaking no English, and nearly blind. Mama didn't know where else she could get work and we had nowhere else to move *to*. On February 25 the choice was made for us. We were given forty-eight hours to clear out.

The secondhand dealers had been prowling around for weeks, like wolves, offering humiliating prices for goods and furniture they knew many of us would have to sell sooner or later. Mama had left all but her most valuable possessions in Ocean Park, simply because she had nowhere to put them. She had brought along her pottery, her silver, heirlooms like the kimonos[23] Granny had brought from Japan, tea sets, lacquered tables, and one fine old set of china, blue and white porcelain, almost translucent. On the day we were leaving, Woody's car was so crammed with boxes and luggage and kids we had just run out of room. Mama had to sell this china.

One of the dealers offered her fifteen dollars for it. She said it was a full setting for twelve and worth at least two hundred. He said fifteen was his top price. Mama started to quiver. Her eyes blazed up at him. She had been packing all night and trying to calm down Granny, who couldn't understand why we were moving again and what all the rush was about. Mama's nerves were shot, and now navy jeeps were patrolling the streets. She didn't say another word. She just glared at this man, all the rage and frustration channeled at him through her eyes.

He watched her for a moment and said he was sure he couldn't pay more than seventeen fifty for that china.

---

[23] kimonos—long, wide-sleeved Japanese robelike dresses worn with a sash called an obi and often elaborately decorated.

She reached into the red velvet case, took out a dinner plate and hurled it at the floor right in front of his feet.

The man leaped back shouting, "Hey! Hey, don't do that! Those are valuable dishes."

Mama took out another dinner plate and hurled it at the floor, then another and another, never moving, never opening her mouth, just quivering and glaring at the retreating dealer, with tears streaming down her cheeks. He finally turned and **scuttled**[24] out the door, heading for the next house. When he was gone she stood there smashing cups and bowls and platters until the whole set lay in scattered blue and white fragments across the wooden floor.

The American Friends Service helped us find a small house in Boyle Heights, another minority ghetto, in downtown Los Angeles, now inhabited briefly by a few hundred Terminal Island refugees. Executive Order 9066 had been signed by President Roosevelt, giving the War Department authority to define military areas in the western states and to exclude from them anyone who might threaten the war effort. There was a lot of talk about **internment**,[25] or moving inland, or something like that in store for all Japanese Americans. I remember my brothers sitting around the table talking very intently about what we were going to do, how we would keep the family together. They had seen how quickly Papa was removed, and they knew now that he would not be back for quite a while. Just before leaving Terminal Island Mama had received her first letter, from Bismarck, North Dakota. He had been imprisoned at Fort Lincoln, in an all-male camp for enemy aliens.

Papa had been the **patriarch**.[26] He had always decided everything in the family. With him gone, my brothers,

---

[24] **scuttled**—scurried; moved quickly.

[25] **internment**—confinement during wartime.

[26] **patriarch**—oldest male and head of the family.

like **councilors**[27] in the absence of a chief, worried about what should be done. The ironic thing is, there wasn't much left to decide. These were mainly days of quiet, desperate waiting for what seemed at the time to be inevitable. There is a phrase the Japanese use in such situations, when something difficult must be endured. You would hear the older heads, the Issei,[28] telling others very quietly, *"Shikata, ga nai."* (It cannot be helped.) *"Shikata ga nai."* (It must be done.)

Mama and Woody went to work packing celery for a Japanese produce dealer. Kiyo and my sister May and I enrolled in the local school, and what sticks in my memory from those weeks is the teacher—not her looks, her remoteness. In Ocean Park my teacher had been a kind, grandmotherly woman who used to sail with us in Papa's boat from time to time and who wept the day we had to leave. In Boyle Heights the teacher felt cold and distant. I was confused by all the moving and was having trouble with the classwork, but she would never help me out. She would have nothing to do with me.

This was the first time I had felt outright hostility from a Caucasian. Looking back, it is easy enough to explain. Public attitudes toward the Japanese in California were shifting rapidly. In the first few months of the Pacific war, America was on the run. Tolerance had turned to distrust and irrational fear. The hundred-year-old tradition of anti-Orientalism on the west coast soon resurfaced, more vicious than ever. Its result became clear about a month later, when we were told to make our third and final move.

The name Manzanar meant nothing to us when we left Boyle Heights. We didn't know where it was or what it was. We went because the government ordered us to.

---

[27] **councilors**—group of people who meet to consult, discuss, or give advice.
[28] Issei—first-generation Japanese immigrants.

And, in the case of my older brothers and sisters, we went with a certain amount of relief. They had all heard stories of Japanese homes being attacked, of beatings in the streets of California towns. They were as frightened of the Caucasians as Caucasians were of us. Moving, under what appeared to be government protection, to an area less directly threatened by the war seemed not such a bad idea at all. For some it actually sounded like a fine adventure.

Our pickup point was a Buddhist church in Los Angeles. It was very early, and misty, when we got there with our luggage. Mama had bought heavy coats for all of us. She grew up in eastern Washington and knew that anywhere inland in early April would be cold. I was proud of my new coat, and I remember sitting on a duffel bag trying to be friendly with the Greyhound driver. I smiled at him. He didn't smile back. He was befriending no one. Someone tied a numbered tag to my collar and to the duffel bag (each family was given a number, and that became our official designation[29] until the camps were closed), someone else passed out box lunches for the trip, and we climbed aboard.

I had never been outside Los Angeles County, never traveled more than ten miles from the coast, had never even ridden on a bus. I was full of excitement, the way any kid would be, and wanted to look out the window. But for the first few hours the shades were drawn. Around me other people played cards, read magazines, dozed, waiting. I settled back, waiting too, and finally fell asleep. The bus felt very secure to me. Almost half its passengers were immediate relatives. Mama and my older brothers had succeeded in keeping most of us together, on the same bus, headed for the same camp. I didn't realize until much later what a job that was. The strategy had been, first, to have everyone living in the

---

[29] **designation**—distinguishing name; identification.

same district when the **evacuation**[30] began, and then to get all of us included under the same family number, even though names had been changed by marriage. Many families weren't as lucky as ours and suffered months of anguish while trying to arrange transfers from one camp to another.

We rode all day. By the time we reached our destination, the shades were up. It was late afternoon. The first thing I saw was a yellow swirl across a blurred, reddish setting sun. The bus was being pelted by what sounded like splattering rain. It wasn't rain. This was my first look at something I would soon know very well, a billowing flurry of dust and sand churned up by the wind through Owens Valley.[31]

We drove past a barbed-wire fence, through a gate, and into an open space where trunks and sacks and packages had been dumped from the baggage trucks that drove out ahead of us. I could see a few tents set up, the first rows of black barracks, and beyond them, blurred by sand, rows of barracks that seemed to spread for miles across this plain. People were sitting on cartons or milling around, with their backs to the wind, waiting to see which friends or relatives might be on this bus. As we approached, they turned or stood up, and some moved toward us expectantly. But inside the bus no one stirred. No one waved or spoke. They just stared out the windows, **ominously**[32] silent. I didn't understand this. Hadn't we finally arrived, our whole family intact? I opened a window, leaned out, and yelled happily. "Hey! This whole bus is full of Wakatsukis!"

Outside, the greeters smiled. Inside there was an explosion of laughter, hysterical, tension-breaking laughter that left my brothers choking and whacking each other across the shoulders.

---

[30] **evacuation**—process of removal from a place in an organized way.

[31] Owens Valley, California, is where the Manzanar detention camp was located.

[32] **ominously**—menacingly; in a way that threatens evil.

QUESTIONS TO CONSIDER

1. How does the narrator's pre-war life in Ocean Park differ from that of the Japanese-American children described later?

2. Why does Papa come to see himself as a "man without a country"?

3. How would you explain the narrator's experiences with and reactions to the children she meets on Terminal Island, and what can be learned from that experience?

4. Why do you think Mama destroys a full set of china?

5. What major decisions does Mama make after Papa leaves, and what is the rationale for her decisions?

from

No-No Boy

BY JOHN OKADA

About a year after World War II began, interned Japanese Americans were given several choices: resettle on the East Coast, work outside the camps, or—for males—join an all-Nisei (second generation Japanese-American) army regiment. Before being released for work or military service, internees were asked two questions: Would you serve in combat wherever ordered? Would you forswear any allegiance to the Japanese emperor? Those who answered "no" to both questions were labeled "no-no boys" and often were sent to prison. John Okada (1923–1971) wrote the story of one such man in his novel, No-No Boy *(1957). In contrast to the title character in his book, Okada served as a sergeant in the United States Air Force during World War II. In the fourteen years before his death,* No-No Boy *failed to sell out the first edition of 1,500 copies, and Okada died certain that his work had met with disfavor. Today, however, it is highly acclaimed. Here, Ichiro, the title character, has returned home after the war to confront his mother's beliefs and his own identity.*

"Ichiro."

He propped himself up on an elbow and looked at her. She had hardly changed. Surely, there must have been a time when she could smile and, yet, he could not remember.

"Yeah?"

"Lunch is on the table."

As he pushed himself off the bed and walked past her to the kitchen, she took broom and dustpan and swept up the mess he had made.

There were eggs, fried with soy sauce, sliced cold meat, boiled cabbage, and tea and rice. They all ate in silence, not even disturbed once by the tinkling of the bell. The father cleared the table after they had finished and dutifully retired to watch the store. Ichiro had smoked three cigarettes before his mother ended the silence.

"You must go back to school."

He had almost forgotten that there had been a time before the war when he had actually gone to college for two years and studiously applied himself to courses in the engineering school. The statement staggered him. Was that all there was to it? Did she mean to sit there and imply that the four **intervening**[1] years were to be casually forgotten and life resumed as if there had been no four years and no war and no Eto who had spit on him because of the thing he had done?

"I don't feel much like going to school."

"What will you do?"

"I don't know."

"With an education, your opportunities in Japan will be unlimited. You must go and complete your studies."

"Ma," he said slowly, "Ma, I'm not going to Japan. Nobody's going to Japan. The war is over. Japan lost. Do you hear? Japan lost."

---

[1] **intervening**—those that came between two points in time.

"You believe that?" It was said in the tone of an adult asking a child who is no longer a child if he really believed that Santa Claus was real.

"Yes, I believe it. I know it. America is still here. Do you see the great Japanese army walking down the streets? No. There is no Japanese army any more."

"The boat is coming and we must be ready."

"The boat?"

"Yes." She reached into her pocket and drew out a worn envelope.

The letter had been mailed from Sao Paulo, Brazil, and was addressed to a name that he did not recognize. Inside the envelope was a single sheet of flimsy, rice paper covered with intricate **flourishes**[2] of Japanese **characters**.[3]

"What does it say?"

She did not bother to pick up the letter. "To you who are a loyal and honorable Japanese, it is with humble and heartfelt joy that I relay this momentous message. Word has been brought to us that the victorious Japanese government is presently making preparations to send ships which will return to Japan those residents in foreign countries who have steadfastly maintained their faith and loyalty to our Emperor. The Japanese government regrets that the responsibilities arising from the victory compels them to delay in the sending of the vessels. To be among the few who remain to receive this honor is a gratifying tribute. Heed not[4] the propaganda of the radio and newspapers which endeavor to convince the people with lies about the allied[5] victory. Especially, heed not the lies of your traitorous countrymen who have turned their backs on the country of their birth and who will suffer

---

[2] **flourishes**—enhancements; embellishments.

[3] **characters**—letters or symbols used in writing or printing.

[4] Heed not—do not listen to nor consider.

[5] allied—refers to the fifty countries in World War II, including the United States, China, Great Britain, and the Soviet Union, who together opposed the Axis powers that included Germany, Italy, Japan and six other countries.

for their treasonous acts. The day of glory is close at hand. The rewards will be beyond our greatest expectations. What we have done, we have done only as Japanese, but the government is grateful. Hold your heads high and make ready for the journey, for the ships are coming."

"Who wrote that?" he asked **incredulously.**[6] It was like a weird nightmare. It was like finding out that an incurable strain of insanity **pervaded**[7] the family, an **intangible**[8] horror that swayed and taunted beyond the grasp of reaching fingers.

"A friend in South America. We are not alone."

"We *are* alone," he said **vehemently.**[9] "This whole thing is crazy. You're crazy. I'm crazy. All right, so we made a mistake. Let's admit it."

"There has been no mistake. The letter confirms."

"Sure it does. It proves there's crazy people in the world besides us. If Japan won the war, what the hell are we doing here? What are you doing running a grocery store? It doesn't figure. It doesn't figure because we're all wrong. The minute we admit that, everything is fine. I've had a lot of time to think about all this. I've thought about it, and every time the answer comes out the same. You can't tell me different any more."

She sighed ever so slightly. "We will talk later when you are feeling better." Carefully folding the letter and placing it back in the envelope, she returned it to her pocket. "It is not I who tell you that the ship is coming. It is in the letter. If you have come to doubt your mother— and I'm sure you do not mean it even if you speak in weakness—it is to be regretted. Rest a few days. Think

---

[6] **incredulously**—with skepticism; unwilling to accept as true.

[7] **pervaded**—spread through; permeated.

[8] **intangible**—incapable of being perceived by the senses; literally, not touchable.

[9] **vehemently**—emotionally; forcefully.

more deeply and your doubts will disappear. You are my son, Ichiro."

No, he said to himself as he watched her part the curtains and start into the store. There was a time when I was your son. There was a time that I no longer remember when you used to smile a mother's smile and tell me stories about gallant and fierce warriors who protected their lords with blades of shining steel and about the old woman who found a peach in the stream and took it home and, when her husband split it in half, a husky little boy tumbled out to fill their hearts with boundless joy. I was that boy in the peach and you were the old woman and we were Japanese with Japanese feelings and Japanese pride and Japanese thoughts because it was all right then to be Japanese and feel and think all the things that Japanese do even if we lived in America. Then there came a time when I was only half Japanese because one is not born in America and raised in America and taught in America and one does not speak and swear and drink and smoke and play and fight and see and hear in America among Americans in American streets and houses without becoming American and loving it. But I did not love enough, for you were still half my mother and I was thereby still half Japanese and when the war came and they told me to fight for America, I was not strong enough to fight you and I was not strong enough to fight the bitterness which made the half of me which was you bigger than the half of me which was America and really the whole of me that I could not see or feel. Now that I know the truth when it is too late and the half of me which was you is no longer there, I am only half of me and the half that remains is American by law because the government was wise and strong enough to know why it was that I could not fight for America and did not strip me of my birthright.[10] But it is not enough to be American only in the eyes of the law and it is not enough to be only half an American and know that it is an empty half. I am not your son and I am not Japanese and I am not American. I can go someplace and tell people that I've got an inverted stomach and that I am an American, true and blue and Hail Columbia, but the army wouldn't have me because of the stomach. That's easy and I would do it, only I've got to convince myself first and that I cannot do. I wish with all my heart that I were Japanese or that I were American. I am neither and I blame you and I blame myself and I blame the world which is made up of many countries which fight with each other and kill and hate and destroy but not enough, so that they must kill and hate and destroy again and again and again. It is so easy and simple that I cannot understand it at all. And the reason I do not understand it is because I do not understand you who were the half of me that is no more and because I do not understand what it was about that half that made me destroy the half of me which was American and the half which might have become the whole of me if I had said yes I will go and fight in your army because that is what I believe and want and cherish and love . . .

Defeatedly, he crushed the stub of a cigarette into an ash tray filled with many other stubs and reached for the package to get another. It was empty and he did not want to go into the store for more because he did not feel much like seeing either his father or mother. He went into the bedroom and tossed and groaned and half slept.

---

[10] strip me of my birthright—take away my United States citizenship.

QUESTIONS TO CONSIDER

1. As the selection opens, what is the situation?

2. In your opinion, how is it possible for Ichiro's mother to believe the letter she receives?

3. Why did Ichiro become a no-no boy?

4. How does Ichiro now regard his decision not to fight for the United States during the war? Why?

5. What external and internal conflicts face Ichiro, and how do you think he might resolve those conflicts?

6. Do you think Ichiro's conflict is unique to him? Why or why not?

from

Filipino American Lives

BY YEN LE ESPIRITU

*When Professor Yen Le Espiritu (1963–   ) began an oral history
of selected members of the San Diego Filipino-American community,
her primary purpose was to "trace the connections between the
life experiences of Filipino Americans and their changing sense
of identities." What she heard was so compelling that she decided
to write a book,* Filipino American Lives *(1995), from which the
two selections here are taken. In the first, Juanita Santos, born in
the Philippines in 1918, marries her husband A. B. after World War II
and comes to the United States. In the second, Connie Tirona, a
second-generation Filipina American born in California in 1929,
marries a navy man who is stationed three times in the Philippines.
Both stories provide a Filipina-American's perspective on
discrimination in the United States.*

Working and Dealing with Racism in San Diego

As soon as we arrived at Mercy Hospital, Sister
Augustine brought me to meet Sister Anna Marie, the

supervisor of the pharmacy, because A. B. had told them that I had a pharmacy degree from the Philippines. So the sister hired me right away! I was very lucky. . . .

In the 1950s, most Americans thought that Filipinos just worked in the kitchen. My first week at Mercy Hospital, I was typing the label for one of the prescriptions. And here came a doctor. He asked me, "Hey, do you know what you are doing?" When I gave him the label, he turned to Sister Anna Marie, my sister supervisor, and said, "Hey, Sister, she knows what she is doing." The sister told him, "Of course, she is just as educated as you are." The next thing he said was, "Are there schools in the Philippines?" I was shocked. I shook my finger at him—he was tall, very handsome, blue eyes—and I said, "You know what, Doctor, you are ignorant. Our University of Santo Tomas is twenty-five years older than your Harvard University." And you know what? Since then, my **inferiority complex**[1]—being short, and very brown, and very Filipino—fell away, because if this educated man is ignorant, what more with the "ordinary" green, yellow, blue man on the street?

Once when I was reading the bulletin board [at Mercy Hospital], a woman came up to me and asked me if I knew how to read. I told her that I did. When she asked where I worked, I pointed to the pharmacy. She apparently did not believe me, because she went to talk to the sister, and when she came out of there, she just looked at me, up and down. But I didn't know that those were prejudices; to me, these people were just ignorant.

Another time, one of the sisters told me, "My child, are you lost? The kitchen is that way." I said, "No, Sister, I work at the pharmacy." At Mercy Hospital, there were some twenty or so Filipino workers in the kitchen. All of them were very nice, devoted family people.

---

[1] **inferiority complex**—pronounced feeling of being not as good as others.

Because of this ignorance, every time there is a Filipino program and I am the master of ceremony, if we have any professional on stage, I will always mention that she is a pharmacist, he is a doctor. . . . The other Filipinos in town used to say that I was prejudiced and that I only recognized professionals. But that was not true. I just wanted to "educate" the other races that the Filipinos are as knowledgeable and cultured as they are. I wanted respect for my people. I wanted to project a positive image of the Filipinos and my native country.

Discrimination in San Diego

When we came back from the Philippines in 1970, my husband was stationed at Camp Pendleton.[2] We bought a house here in Carlsbad. I think we were among the first Filipinos to move to Carlsbad. It's still a very white community.

When we first moved here, my son would always go jogging. One time, he was running through the neighborhood. A police car stopped him, "What are you doing in this neighborhood?" "I live here." "No, you don't." He said, "Well, I live at this address. But I am not going to ride in the car with you. You can follow me home." So they followed him home to make sure that he lived there. I always tell my children, "It's going to happen to you. Don't ever resist the police."

In the last fifteen years, I think things have simmered down. I don't run into prejudices or people looking at me cross-eyed that often any more. But it still happens. My daughter, Lori, when she was giving birth at Tri-City Hospital, was having a difficult time, as it was going to be a breech delivery.[3] And they were just waiting for the baby to turn.

---

[2] Camp Pendleton—a United States Marine base located north of San Diego, California.

[3] breech delivery—in childbirth, a difficult delivery, where the baby is positioned to be born bottom or feet first rather than headfirst.

The doctor was in another part of the hospital. Well, another shift of nurses had come on. I knew the first shift, because some of them were friends and classmates of our children. Before the first shift left, I asked them to get the doctor, because I didn't think the baby was going to turn and Lori's labor was nearing almost thirty hours. I said, "I think you should get that doctor or let me find him."

A nurse from the incoming shift came in. She looked at my daughter, and she looked at me and said, "Do . . . you . . . speak . . . English?" I was very tired and very angry so I said, "Much better than you." And I said, "I would like to speak to the head nurse." I told my daughter she was going to be all right, as I was going to get that doctor right away.

I went to the head nurse and I said, "My daughter has been in labor for almost thirty hours, and I don't appreciate having someone come up to me and ask me if I speak English. I want that doctor right now!" And they got that doctor so fast. I told her, "Is it because we are of color that you think that we are like rabbits that give birth? I think that nurse is prejudiced." Now, all you have to do is say that word. So, apologies were given. And I said, "You should take a sensitivity course[4] on how to deal with people of color."

The head nurse was a friend of mine, she said, "Oh, gosh! I am so sorry." I said, "It's only because you know me. Why is it that you have to know me? Why isn't everybody made aware?" And so after that incident, they started sensitivity courses there at the hospital. So you have to complain. If you sit back and don't say anything, they tend to walk all over you. And I think for the most part, Filipinos have a **colonial**[5] mentality. They

---

[4] sensitivity course—series of classes designed to increase awareness and understanding of the needs and emotions of other people.

[5] **colonial**—dependent; not used to making decisions on their own behalf.

tend to not do anything. But you don't have to scream at them. You can be calm about it.

Sometimes, I am not sure what it means to be an American. I am not equal to anyone. My color is different and that has mattered all of my life. I feel that not all Americans are equal; they are not. I think when I went to the Philippines, that's when my feelings probably started. I found out that I had to tell these American servicemen that I was an American, and even then they questioned how I became an American. Did I live with an American to become an American? And I think that's when I felt that the word "American" really didn't mean anything if you were a person of color, you know, it really doesn't. I don't know, maybe a lot of people would disagree with me, but that's how I feel. I probably have people say, "Well, then, why doesn't she go back where she came from?"

QUESTIONS TO CONSIDER

1. What is similar about these two accounts and what conclusions might you draw from the similarities?

2. What kinds of stereotyped assumptions were made about these women, and how does each one define herself?

3. How does each woman negotiate racial discrimination, in terms of both her direct responses and her interpretation of the situations she encounters?

4. What changes in attitudes toward Filipinos do the women say has changed? In your opinion, is the situation the same today?

Working

▲

A worker at an Alaskan salmon cannery cleans fish before sealing them in cans.

◀ **Fish Industry** Fishermen off the Gulf of Alaska weather cold temperatures and rough water to make a living.

Building America Chinese laborers take a break during the building of the Northern Pacific Railroad. Over 1,500 Chinese helped to complete the construction.
▼

▲

A Laotian family sorts shrimp on a Texas dock.

Farm Work Harvesters in Hawaii gather pineapples on one of the largest pineapple plantations on the island.

▼

▲
Women cut down sugarcane on the Hawaiian island of Maui.

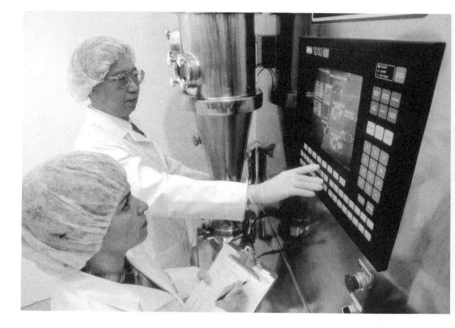

▲

Technology Industry Two technicians manufacture
drugs at a lab.

▲
Education A math teacher
stands before the blackboard.

Medicine A surgeon checks
a needle. ▶

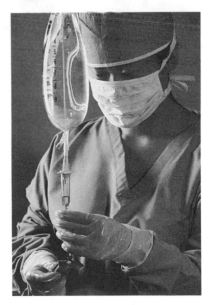

▲

Athletics Professional ice skater Kristi Yamaguchi salutes the audience after her routine. Yamaguchi won a gold medal for the United States at the Olympic Games in Albertville, France, in 1992.

Chinese-American tennis champion Michael Chang has aced his way to victories and gained a worldwide reputation as a skilled competitor. Here, Chang delivers a fierce backhand to his opponent.

▲

Entertainment India-born screenwriter and director M. Night Shyamalan won critical success for his 1999 film, *The Sixth Sense*. The movie was the second highest money earner of 1999.

Examining Relationships

Grandmother

BY CYNTHIA KADOHATA

Cynthia Kadohata has written In the Heart of the Valley of Love, The Floating World, *and* The Glass Mountains. *Her stories also have appeared in* The New Yorker *and* The Pennsylvania Review. *For many years after World War II, some Japanese Americans had difficulty finding work, which often forced them to travel from one place to another. Kadohata refers to this nomadic life as a "floating world," the title of her 1989 autobiographical first novel. In the following excerpt from that coming-of-age story, narrator Olivia Ann describes her contentious relationship with her maternal grandmother.*

My grandmother has always been my tormentor. My mother said she'd been a young woman of spirit; but she was an old woman of fire. In her day it had been considered scandalous for young Japanese women to smoke, but she smoked cigars. Once, when she got especially angry, she took a piece of damp cosmetic cotton and placed it on my ankle so I would hear the sizzle of cotton and think it was skin burning. Later *she* cried. Of the four of us kids, I thought she liked me least. My mother said she didn't dislike me but just expected more of me because I was the oldest.

My grandmother surprised my family by dying one night in a motel in California. Neither of my three brothers liked her any more than I did, and none of us cried at the funeral. My grandmother used to box our ears whenever she pleased, and liked to predict ghastly futures for all of us. We traveled a great deal, and sometimes in the car she talked on and on, until even my mother became annoyed and told her to keep it *down*, just as if she were one of us kids. When she got mad she cursed me. "May you grow hair on your nose!" she would say, and I would run to check a mirror.

Her name was Hisae Fujiitano, a name sort of partway between mine and those of my ancestors. You can trace some of the changes in my family through the changes in our names. In 1875, for the first time, the parents of all my great-grandparents took family names: Yanagita, Osaka (my father's name), Nambu, Takeda, and four Satōs. Before the 1870s, most commoners in Japan were not allowed family names. When the names finally were allowed, sometimes everybody in a village was ordered to take the same one: thus the four Satōs. My mother's mother was born Satō Hisae[1] in a village of Satōs. But though Hisae was her given name, my great-grandparents called her Shimeko, which isn't a real name. "Shimeru" means "to close." They called her Shimeko because she was their eighth child and they hoped that from then on my great-grandmother's womb would be closed.

When Hisae's family came to the United States, her father changed their name to go with their new life. The new name was Fujiitano. Fujii had been the richest man my great-grandfather had ever known, and Itano the happiest. Years later, in Hawaii at the start of World

---

[1] In Japan, as well as in China and Korea, the given name comes after the last, or family, name.

War II, the local school made my grandparents change their children's first names before they could enroll. Satoru, Yukiko, Mariko, Haruko, and Sadamu became Roger, Lily, Laura, Ann, and Roy. Today their original names are just shadows following them. My brothers and I all have American names: Benjamin Todd, Walker Roy, Peter Edward, and me, Olivia Ann.

Before my grandmother died, she told me everything about herself. Sometimes, sitting next to me, she might suddenly grab my hair and pull me over to tell me one more fact about herself: how she had never seen a book until she was twelve, or how she had never cut her long, long hair. She lived with us after her third husband died. But my brothers and I were way ahead of her. Right before she moved in, we gave her a neck chain with a bell attached so we would always hear her approaching and could hide before she reached us. We bought her the bell one Christmas, and she always wore it.

My grandmother liked to tell us about herself during evenings while we all sat talking in front of the motels or houses we stayed at. We were traveling then in what she called ukiyo, the floating world. The floating world was the gas station attendants, restaurants, and jobs we depended on, the motel towns floating in the middle of fields and mountains. In old Japan, ukiyo meant the districts full of brothels,[2] teahouses, and public baths, but it also referred to change and the pleasures and loneliness change brings. For a long time, I never exactly thought of us as part of any of that, though. *We* were stable, traveling through an unstable world while my father looked for jobs.

It seemed as if we were always the only family at the motels we stayed at, and the **proprietors**[3] often gave my brothers and me candy, matches, or gum. We saved most

---

[2] brothels—houses of prostitution.

[3] **proprietors**—owners.

of what we got, and sometimes as my grandmother told stories we would make trades with each other: matches for gum, candy for matches. I had a special piece of chocolate that I'd had for three years and would never trade. Sometimes I licked it, for luck.

My grandmother owned a **valise**[4] in which she carried all her possessions, but the stories she told were also possessions. The stories were fantastic, yet I believed them. She said that when she was young fireflies had invaded her town, so the whole town was lighted even during the nighttime. She said she had been told that the summer she was born, strange clouds passed through the sky. Every night for seven nights, a different cloud. The clouds all had a strange glow, as if someone had taken the moon and stretched it into a cloud shape. Those seven moon-clouds, she said, had been a lucky **omen**.[5] As she spoke, she always gestured a great deal, so the background to her stories would be the soft tinkling of the bell we had bought her.

She did most of the talking, but once in a while one of my parents spoke up to **amplify**[6] or to make their own, new contributions. Other times, my parents might gently indicate that she should stop talking because it was our bedtime, or because they did not approve of the subject. No matter—if she wanted to tell me something she would seek me out later. She would run after me, shouting her facts: I had a white dog! I broke my leg three times! My first husband and I had sex in a public bathroom!

Sometimes my father did seasonal farming work and my mother helped out, but mostly he found work as a body-and-fender man or a carpenter. We sometimes traveled in the Pacific states with one or two other

---

[4] **valise**—small suitcase.

[5] **omen**—sign foretelling a future event.

[6] **amplify**—add to; make more complete.

young Japanese families, heading for jobs the fathers had heard of. We moved often for three reasons. One was bad luck—the businesses my father worked for happened to go under, or the next job we headed to evaporated while we were **in transit.**[7] Also, it could be hard even into the fifties and sixties for Japanese to get good jobs. Nothing was ever quite the position my father felt he deserved. The third reason was that my parents were dissatisfied with their marriage, and, somehow, moving seemed to give **vent**[8] to that dissatisfaction. It was always hard to leave our homes, but once we started traveling, a part of me loved that life. All the packing and moving was especially hard on my parents, but I think even they enjoyed some of the long drives—at least, they did when my grandmother was quiet. I remember how fine it was to drive through the passage of light from morning to noon to night.

What I learned, traveling in Oregon, Wyoming, California, and Washington, was that my first grandfather had drowned off the coast of Honolulu. My third, I knew, had died of old age. My grandmother said she was still married when she met her third husband. She had been trying to fix him up with a woman from Japan, but he decided he wanted to marry her instead. He begged her to leave her second husband, and she couldn't resist his begging.

"You couldn't resist because you loved him so much?" I said. "You couldn't resist because he was so handsome?"

"I couldn't resist because his begging was like buzzing in my ears," she said. "I had to make it stop." She hit one of her ears as if to stop some buzzing.

Actually, it was my mother, one evening when we were in northern California, who told me her father had

---

[7] **in transit**—in the process of moving.

[8] **vent**—a means of escape.

drowned. We were staying at a place someone had lent us while my father had a temporary job helping a friend build a farmhouse. When he finished with this job, we would be on our way to Arkansas, where my father was going to buy into a garage another friend of his owned. "It'll be the first time I've ever owned anything big," he said. "A car don't count."

I was sitting on the porch with my mother and brothers. My father had already gone inside to take a shower and go to bed, and my grandmother was napping.

"Olivia, go get Obāsan," said my mother. "It's pretty out here. She should see." Two Japanese words for "grandmother" are "obāsan" and "obāchan." You call your grandmother Obāsan if you're not close to her, Obāchan if you are. I think my mother would have liked for us to call our grandmother Obāchan, but we never did. We called her Obāsan. My father wanted us to call her Grandma—more American.

Ben and Walker looked at me. We took daily turns dealing with Obāsan. Ben was eight, four years younger than I; Walker was seven; and Peter, two. Ben was the opposite of Walker, outgoing and talkative where Walker was quiet and brooding. I was sort of outgoing and quiet both, depending.

"I think it's Ben's turn," I said.

His jaw dropped in outrage. "No. Remember, I gave you gum and you said you would take my turn."

He was right—I had the gum in my mouth. I tried to swallow it and almost choked. So I went inside. The house was one room. The light was very low, barely good enough to read in, and the room was smoky from my grandmother's cigars.

"What do you want?" said Obāsan.

She took an **ominous**[9] step toward me with her cigar and I got scared and ran. When I got outside and saw my

---

[9] **ominous**—alarming; threatening.

mother, I remembered she'd wanted me to get my grandmother. So I turned around and shouted as loudly as I could, "Mom wants you!" When I saw her at the door I turned to my mother, who was standing right next to me. "She's coming," I said.

"Goodness," said my mother.

My grandmother sat outside with us, and after a while, when I'd decided she was in a good mood, I asked her whether she'd cried for weeks after her first and third husbands died.

"Does a slave cry when the master dies?"

"It depends," I said. "Did you love any of your husbands?"

She paused, and I could see that she had loved one of them. But she didn't say so. She said, "I loved all of them in a way, and none of them in a way."

"So why get married?"

"Because they asked." I knew that Japanese women were nothing without husbands, and she probably had not wanted to be nothing.

"I remember the day my father drowned," said my mother. We always got extra quiet when my mother spoke. This was the first I'd heard of any drowning. My mother rarely initiated small talk, and usually when she spoke she had something she especially wanted to say. She had an elegant, **lush**[10] face, and always had about her a slight air of being disoriented, as if she could not quite remember how she came to be wherever she was. I think sometimes people interpreted that disoriented air as **aloofness**.[11] "When I found out what had happened to him, I went outside and wandered around for hours, and I found a wooden rose in a field. It had the look, texture, and strength of a piece of carved wood, but it was a real flower. It was alive.

---

[10] **lush**—extremely pleasing to the senses.

[11] **aloofness**—being distant emotionally; being reserved and remote; being above it all.

I've never found a reference to a wooden rose in books on flowers, but I'm sure it existed. I remember thinking it was impossible, just like my father's death was impossible. For a few hours, I was in another realm, and impossible things happened."

The house my father had been working on sat way in the distance. The family would be moving there the following week. Fireflies hovered around the house, but they weren't the fireflies of my grandmother's childhood invasion. They blinked like Christmas lights. They made the house seem enchanted. I thought how lucky some children would be to live in a place like that.

My grandmother pushed my head down suddenly so that the side of my face was pressed against the concrete porch. "Be careful you never marry anyone who's going to die young," she said.

I tried to say okay, but my mouth was being squished by her hand, so I said, "Uh-keh."

She let me go and wiped her nose with the back of her hand. I sat up and saw my big wad of gum sitting on the porch. I dusted it off, plunked it into my mouth, and blew a big bubble to show my grandmother she didn't bother me. In truth, I was shaking inside. But anyway I thought I had found out something I'd wanted to know—it was her first husband she'd loved. I liked finding out things about her. I just wished it weren't such hard work.

QUESTIONS TO CONSIDER

1. Why is Olivia both fascinated and repelled by her grandmother?

2. Why do you think Olivia's grandmother carries her stories like "possessions"?

3. Why is Olivia so interested in determining which husband her grandmother most loved?

4. How is Olivia caught between generations and cultures?

5. In what ways do Olivia and her grandmother connect?

6. Why would living in a "floating world" be difficult for any family but especially difficult for an immigrant family?

from

Vedi

BY VED MEHTA

*Ved Mehta (1934–   ) has worked as a journalist, novelist, travel
writer, autobiographer, and staff writer for The New Yorker
magazine. He was born into a doctor's family in Lahore, then an
Indian city that is now a part of Pakistan. At the age of three, he
contracted meningitis and lost his eyesight. His father, fearing he
would face a future in poverty, sent him over 1,000 miles away to
Bombay, India, to be educated at the Dadar School for the Blind.
Ironically, the school had been established for poor orphans, the
very population his father feared his son would join. However, the
director, Ras Mohun, was American-trained, a fact that impressed
Vedi's father. Vedi remained at the school for the next four years.
Conditions were quite cruel, he was often very sick with disease,
and he received a mediocre education at best. Initially, he stayed
with the Mohuns and their daughter Heea, calling the Mohuns
Auntie and Uncle as terms of respect. In this selection Mehta
describes his relationship with a fellow student, Deoji, an older,
partially-sighted boy.*

After I had stayed with Mr. and Mrs. Ras Mohun for a week, Mrs. Ras Mohun said to me at dinner, "Our sleeping quarters are too small. You'll be better off staying in the boys' dormitory with the other fellows."

"Shouldn't we really write to Dr. Mehta first?" Mr. Ras Mohun asked.

"Dr. Mehta is well-to-do," Mrs. Ras Mohun said. "If he knew the size of our sleeping quarters, he would understand."

"The beds in the boys' dormitory are not suitable for a well-to-do boy," Mr. Ras Mohun said. "But I suppose we can provide for a special bed for Vedi. Of course, he will continue to take his breakfast, lunch, tiffin,[1] and dinner with us in our sitting-and-dining room. I suppose that if he is to amount to anything he must live with the other blind boys. The worst thing that can happen to blind children is to have overfond care."

"Where is it?" I said. "I don't want to go there."

"It's just through the door," Mr. Ras Mohun said. "The boys' dormitory is on this side of our sitting-and-dining room, beyond the boys' staircase, which you go up and down. The girls' dormitory is on the other side, beyond the girls' staircase."

"I'll stay upstairs with Heea," I said.

A day or two after this conversation, Mr. Ras Mohun took my hand and walked me a few steps from the sitting-and-dining room to the boys' dormitory, on the other side of the boys' staircase. Here he called over a boy who was twice my height, and said, "Vedi, this is your loving big brother Deoji. He will look after you."

I clung to Mr. Ras Mohun's leg. "He is not my brother!" I cried. "I want to stay with Heea."

Mr. Ras Mohun shook his leg free. I heard the click-click of his retreating footsteps. Before I could run after

---

[1] tiffin—an Anglo-Indian word that originally meant *lunch*. Here it refers to tea, a late-afternoon meal of sandwiches, scones and/or cake, and milk or tea.

him, I heard the crashing sound of the metal accordion gate being closed, and he was gone.

Deoji bent down and pulled my cheeks—he had small, cold hands—and said, in faltering Hindustani,[2] "What nice fat cheeks you have. You must come from the house of very well-to-do people."

. . .

He sat me down on a sort of platform a little way inside the room.

"What is this?" I asked, running my hands all around the platform. It consisted of a few bare boards laid side by side on top of a heavy iron frame.

"This is my bed. You can play on it. You don't have a bed yet, but they are going to bring one. It's going to be a special spring bed[3] with a mosquito net."

Deoji showed me around the boys' dormitory. It was a long room lined with two rows of beds like his, with a narrow passageway between.

Suddenly, there were the shouts and rough laughter of boys running into the room.

Deoji said something to them in Marathi.

"Hold him up!" a few boys shouted, in broken Hindustani. "Let the partially sighted see!"

Deoji lifted me up and then put me down.

Many boys scrambled forward and touched me all over. They kept touching my cheeks.

"What fat cheeks he has!" one exclaimed.

"How round his cheeks are!" someone else said.

A boy started tugging at my clothes. "His clothes are soft and pressed."

Deoji tried to push the boys along, but they wouldn't move.

---

[2] Hindustani—the language of northern India. Deoji speaks in faltering, or hesitant, Hindustani because it is not his native dialect, Marath.

[3] spring bed—bed with a mattress with springs.

Several of the boys clasped my hands in their rough ones.

"What soft hands he has!" one boy said.

"He has soft hands like a girl's," another said.

One boy caught hold of both my hands and exclaimed, "So smooth! Never had to work!" His **rasping**[4] fingers went over my hands again and again, in disbelief. "What is your name?"

"Vedi."

"Vedi! A nickname for Ved?"

"Yes," I said.

"He's called that because he's small," someone else said.

I tried to pull away. The boy holding both my hands laughed and tightened his grip. "Why don't you laugh?" he suddenly asked me.

Everyone laughed.

"Leave him alone," Deoji said. "He's Mr. Ras Mohun's personal guest. Didn't you all hear how gently Mr. Ras Mohun spoke to him in the classroom yesterday?"

I heard again the clicking sound of Mr. Ras Mohun's shoes. "Mr. Shoes," someone said.

The boy let my hands drop. Everyone stepped back. There was an uneasy silence as the shoes clicked louder and louder. At that moment, I realized that since I entered the boys' dormitory I had heard the sound of no other shoes—only the sound of bare feet shuffling.

That evening, a special bed was wheeled in for me, and it was very different not only from the other boys' platformlike beds but also from the cots I had slept on at home and upstairs, in Mr. and Mrs. Ras Mohun's sleeping quarters. It had a smooth metal frame with railings at the head and the foot, metal poles from which a mosquito net

---

[4] **rasping**—rough.

was strung, a heavy mattress, and springs. It was placed between Deoji's bed and the corner bed, which was just inside the door and belonged to the Sighted Master. The Sighted Master was the head of the boys' dormitory and the only completely sighted person there.

The boys immediately **dubbed**[5] my bed "the hospital bed." I didn't like the bed, and didn't want to get into it, even though it was bedtime. But Deoji lifted me in and tucked the mosquito net under the edges of the mattress.

. . .

I couldn't go to sleep. My bed was a little longer than the other beds and stuck out into the passageway, so the boys kept bumping into it as they went to the bathroom and came back.

I heard the sound of the metal accordion gate opening and the click-click of Mr. Ras Mohun's shoes. He walked energetically, as if he were saying to himself, "Left, right, left," and yet his step was so light that he might have been Mamaji[6] in high heels. I heard the boys falling on top of their wooden beds, and in a moment the whole boys' dormitory was quiet.

"No one should make any noise," Mr. Ras Mohun said, in his shrill voice, coming in and flicking off the light switch, just like Mamaji at home. "I don't want to have to punish anyone with my ruler. I see the Sighted Master is already asleep." He left.

The bed was so big; the room was so large and so crowded. I cried. I slept. I woke up. All around, people were snoring and grinding their teeth. I pressed my face against the pillow to stop my howls.

I felt someone cautiously untucking the mosquito net.

I held my breath and lay very still. I thought that it was the Sighted Master, and that he was going to punish me. But he was snoring on the other side of my bed.

---

[5] **dubbed**—named; called.

[6] Mamaji—Mother; the northern Indian suffix, -ji, is a term of respect.

Someone put his head inside the mosquito net, and I heard Deoji's voice. "Vedi," he murmured.

I cried into the pillow and clung to it.

"The other boys will hear you," he said. "What will they think?"

He gathered me up with the pillow and carried me out of the boys' dormitory. He sat down on the top step of the boys' staircase, clumsily put me down next to him, and said, in a whisper, "You're only homesick. You miss your mummy. I cried, too, when they first brought me here. I missed my Foundling Home.[7] But I soon forgot about it. In a few days, you'll forget about your mummy, and you'll like it here. We have a swing and a seesaw and climbing bars here. Are you good at climbing?"

"Where are they? I want to see."

"They're outside, in the back courtyard. It's night, and snakes will be out there now. I'll show you those things tomorrow." He pulled my cheeks.

I touched his face. It felt thin and **taut**[8] and rough. I shrank back.

He laughed and pulled my cheeks again and asked me, "What do you call them in Punjabi?"

"*Galls*," I said, laughing. The Punjabi word sounded very funny in front of Deoji.

"Say in Punjabi, 'I have a new loving big brother named Deoji.'"

"I don't want to."

"Please do."

I said it, and he repeated it after me.

"You sound like a duck," I said, and we both laughed.

"No, it is Mr. Ras Mohun who sounds like a duck," he said, in a barely audible whisper. We laughed even more.

"Why do you call Uncle Mr. Ras Mohun?" I asked.

---

[7] Foundling Home—orphanage. Foundlings are children whose unknown parents have deserted them.

[8] **taut**—tightly drawn; stiff; tense.

"I'm too poor to call him Uncle. Besides, I don't have any uncles. I have no family, no relations. I am solitary."

"Who was it you stayed with when you were small?"

"I stayed with my missionary mummy and daddy."

"What are missionaries?"

"Missionaries? Missionaries? Well, you can say they are like Mr. and Mrs. Ras Mohun. Mr. and Mrs. Ras Mohun are your missionary uncle and auntie."

"How did you find your missionary mummy and daddy?"

"They told me that I had come to them as a little baby and that they had named me Deoji. Now I'm fifteen. I've been here for seven years. My missionary mummy and daddy sent me to this school when I was already eight."

"Where are your missionary mummy and daddy?"

"In their mission orphanage."

"Can I—"

"Sh-h-h. We've broken a strict rule by leaving the boys' dormitory. If the Sighted Master finds out and reports us, Mr. Ras Mohun will beat us with his ruler."

He took my hand, and we tiptoed back.

QUESTIONS TO CONSIDER

1. Why do Auntie and Uncle send Vedi to sleep in the boys' dormitory?

2. In what ways do the boys become familiar with Vedi? How do these methods differ from how sighted people meet each other?

3. What do you predict Vedi will learn from his association with Deoji and the other students? What personal characteristics do you think will help Mehta to survive?

4. How does Mehta describe everything in this piece? What is missing, and why?

5. How is this story similar to that of any person trying to get his or her bearings in a "foreign country"?

Authors

▲
Maxine Hong Kingston

▲
Shawn Wong

▲
Amy Tan

▲
Cynthia Kadohata

▲

John Okada

▲

Janice Mirikitani and Reverend Cecil Williams join hands with former Senator Bill Bradley (center) during services at the Glide Memorial United Methodist Church in San Francisco.

Ms.

BY JANICE MIRIKITANI

Janice Mirikitani (c. 1942–   ), a third-generation Japanese American, was just an infant when her family was shipped to a Japanese-American internment camp in Arkansas during World War II. They remained there until she was three. Today, Mirikitani is a choreographer, community activist, artist, and feminist. In 1999 she was awarded the Asian American Arts Foundation Golden Ring Award, given to artists who promote Asian Pacific arts and increase cross-cultural dialogue. In her poetry, including Shedding Silence *(1987), Mirikitani is best known for her striking imagery and for her focus on social issues. In this poem published in* We, the Dangerous: New and Selected Poems *by Janice Mirikitani (1995), she rebukes a woman for her reaction to being called "Miss."*

I got into a thing
with someone
because I called her
miss ann/hearst/rockerfeller/hughes
instead of ms.

I said
it was a waste of time
worrying about it.

Her lips pressed white
thinning words like pins
pricking me—a victim of **sexism**.[1]

I wanted to
call her what
she deserved
but knowing it would please her
instead
I said,

>   white lace & satin was never soiled by sexism
>   sheltered as you are by mansions built on Indian
>   land

>   your diamonds shipped with slaves from Africa
>   your underwear washed by Chinese launderies
>   your house cleaned by my grandmother

so do not push me any further.

>   And when you quit
>   killing us
>   for democracy
>   and stop calling ME *gook*,

>   I will call you
whatever you like.

---

[1] **sexism**—discrimination on the basis of gender.

QUESTIONS TO CONSIDER

1. Why does the speaker identify the "someone" as "miss ann/hearst/rockerfeller/hughes"?

2. In stanza three, what sound devices help to accentuate the meaning of the poem?

3. Do you think the focus of this poem (and the speaker's criticism) is sexism or is it something else?

4. What are miss ann's choices in responding, and what do you think she has the opportunity to learn?

5. What might the speaker understand from miss ann over time?

6. Upon what common ground might the two women begin to establish a respectful relationship?

Toussaint LaRue

BY GUS LEE

Gus Lee (1946–   ) was born to immigrant parents who fled China and settled in the Panhandle, a primarily African-American district in San Francisco. In 1976, Lee earned his law degree. He began writing in 1989 when his daughter requested that he write their family history. The semi-autobiographical China Boy *(1991) was widely praised, and in 1993 Lee became a full-time writer. In this excerpt, the protagonist Kai Ting, who has been regularly beaten up by some of the neighborhood boys, is befriended by Toussaint, who tries to explain the theory of fights and why Kai should fight back.*

A rail-thin nine-year-old named Toussaint LaRue looked on during these beatings and only hit me once. I therefore assumed that he occupied some lower social **niche**[1] than mine. Like a snail's.

He took no pleasure in the China Boy rituals. He instead talked to me. I suspected that he had devised a new method of pain infliction.

---

[1] **niche**—place; compartment.

"Toussaint," he said, offering his hand. "Ya'lls supposed ta shake it." He grinned when I put my hand out with the same enthusiasm with which I would pet Mr. Carter's bulldog. Toussaint, like Evil, had a big gap between his front teeth.

Toussaint would become my guide to American boyhood.

My primary bond to him was for the things he did not do. He did not pound or trap me. He never cut me down. Or laughed with knives in his eyes. Then he opened his heart by explaining things to me, giving me his learning, and taking me into his home.

"China. Don be cryin no mo'. Don work on dis here block, no sir, Cap'n! Give 'er up. When ya'll cry, hol' it insida yo'self. Shif' yo' feet an air-out, go park-side. Preten ya'll gone fishin. Don run, now. Ain't cool."

"Fish in park?" I asked.

"Cheez! Ya'll don colly[2] nothin! Ferget da fish, China. Dry yo' tears."

He told me about the theory of fights. That kids did it because it was how you became a man later on.

"Momma tole me," he said, "in ole days, no Negro man kin hit or fight. We belongs to da whites, like hosses.

"Man fight 'notha man, be damagin white man goods. So he get whipped. An I mean *whipped*." He shook his head and rubbed the top of it, easing the pain of the thought.

"Now, ain't no mo' dat," he said, smiling. "We kin fights, like men." He was speaking very seriously. Fighting was a measure of citizenship. Of civilization. I didn't think so.

"China, stan up."

"Why?" I whined.

"Putchur fists up. Make a fist! Right. Bof han's."

---

[2] colly—(slang) understand.

"Dis one—," he said, holding my left. "It fo' guardin yo' face. Dis here one—dats fo' poundin da fool who call ya out. Here come a punch, and ya'll block it. China—you listenin ta me?"

"No fight, no reason!" I said hotly.

"No reason!?" he yelled. "You can fight wif no *reason?* Boy! Whatchu *talkin* about?"

Uh-oh, I thought. Toussaint's hands were on his hips.

"Evera kid on dis here block like ta knock you upside da head and make you *bleed* and ya'll got no *reason?* China. Ain't no dude in da Handle got mo' cause fo' fightin *evera* day den *you!*"

"Too many boy fight," I said, drawing back from his heat.

"Uh-*uh!* No sir, Cap'n! Big-time nossir! Lissen. Some kids, dey fight *hard.* But ain't *never* gonna be no gangin up on one kid. *Dat* ain't cool." He shook his head. "Kid stan on his feet. No one else feet. Ain't *nobody* gonna stan inaway a dat. An youse best colly dat."

"Hittin' long," I tried.

"Say what?" he said.

"Long. Not light!"

"Wrong? Ya'll sayin fightin's *wrong?*"

"Light," I said.

"Howzat?"

"Bad yuing chi," I explained.

"Say *what?*"

"Bad, uh, karma!" I said, finding the East Indian word often used by my sisters.

"Well, China, ya'll thinks awful funny. Don have nothin ta do wif no *caramels.* No matta Big Willie take yo' candies. Ain't *candies.* It not bein *chicken.* Not bein yella. Ya'll don havta like it. Sakes, China, no one like ta Fist City. Well, maybe Big Willie, he like it. But like it or don like it, no matter none. Ya'll jus *do* it."

He invited me to play in his house. Many of the games involved capturing cockroaches. "Ya'll ready?"

he would ask, and I would nod, nervously. Toos would kick the wall next to the sink, and roaches would slither out of the dust and the cracked plaster. Toos would use his plastic cup, smacking it quickly onto the floor, smiling as he watched the captured roach's antennae struggle to escape, its hard body clicking angrily against the plastic.

He made his closest buddies tolerate me. His mother took me to the church of Reverend Jones on Sundays until Edna changed my religion. The simple presence of his company, and that of his pals, saved me from innumerable trashings and gave me time to breathe.

I had never had a friend before, and I cared for him as few lads have for another. My heart fills now when I think of him. That will never change.

QUESTIONS TO CONSIDER

1. How do the style and tone of this selection add to an understanding of the piece?

2. In what ways are Toussaint and Kai alike in your opinion?

3. How does Lee's use of dialect for both Toussaint and Kai contribute to your understanding of the characters?

4. What, according to this selection, is it like to grow up as a member of a minority group in a neighborhood?

5. What values and "rules to live by" does each boy attempt to teach the other, and what values might they have in common?

6. Years later, why do you think Lee feels such affection and deep gratitude for Toussaint?

My Mother Juggling Bean Bags

BY JAMES MITSUI

James Masao Mitsui (1940–   ) grew up in Odessa, a small wheat-farming community in eastern Washington state. He and his sister were the total minority in the school system. A teacher in the Renton, Washington, public schools for thirty-four years, Mitsui published his first volume of poetry, Journal of the Sun, *in 1974. His most recent publication,* From a Three-Cornered World, *was published in 1997. In the following poem, Mitsui celebrates laughter and the closeness of family.*

Laughter is the shortest distance between two people.

—*Victor Borge*

At 71, my mother juggled three,
even four bean bags
while shouting *"yeeaaat"*[1]

and *"yoi-cho"*[2] between her gold
front teeth. My children
stooped to pick up

her mistakes. They watched,
mouths shaped like little *o's,*
as "Little Grandma"

laughed in a language
anyone could understand.
On visitation weekends

we visited her low-income apartment
and shared 7-Up, too many
British jelly cookies

and potato chips.
Now, over twenty years later,
I value my mother's humor.

As a child I had one-present
Christmases, but there was always
roast turkey on holidays,

jeans with no holes, and a first-base
glove from Montgomery Ward
that they really couldn't afford.

---

[1] *yeeaaat*—an exuberant expression in Japanese that is akin to saying an emphatic "Yes!" when we do something right.

[2] *yoi-cho*—a Japanese expression associated with exerting an effort, especially as part of a group, similar to saying "one, two, three!" in English.

I remember the night when two girls
from the Class of '59
had driven ten miles from Odessa

just to show my mother how to
short-sheet my bed. I can still hear
her laughter in the dark.

I can also remember my mother
chasing me with a stick of firewood
around the trash burner in the parlor,

using my father's railroad swear words.
She always managed not
to catch me. Now I warn my children—

when I turn 71, I may turn from poetry
to juggling oranges. I owe it to my mother;
I owe it to my six grandchildren.

QUESTIONS TO CONSIDER

1. What details in the poem tell you something about the family's economic situation when Mitsui was growing up?

2. Why do you think it has taken Mitsui "over twenty years" to value his mother's humor?

3. How do Mitsui's children—another generation—relate to their grandmother?

4. Why is laughter important?

5. How do you think family ties can remain strong through generations when families span two different cultures?

The Lemon Tree Billiards House

BY CEDRIC YAMANAKA

When Cedric Yamanaka (1963–   ) was growing up in a working-class neighborhood of Honolulu, Hawaii, he thought about one day becoming a quarterback for the Dallas Cowboys or a drummer in a rock group. Becoming a writer was far from his mind. By 1986, however, he had won the Ernest Hemingway Memorial Award for Creative Writing, and a year later he received a creative writing fellowship to attend Boston University. In 1996, the film adaptation of the following short story won the award for best Hawaiian film at the Hawaii International Film Festival. In this humorous story, Mitch and Locust Cordero, two very unlikely friends, learn that the way to overcome fear is to face it.

The Lemon Tree Billiards[1] House is on the first floor of an old concrete building on King Street, between

---

[1] Billiards—any number of games played on a rectangular table with a tapered wooden stick, called a *cue*, and wooden balls. Players hit a ball with the cue, driving it and others into one of the pockets located at the four corners or in the middle of the table's two sides.

Aloha Electronics and Uncle Phil's Flowers. The building is old and the pool hall isn't very large—just nine tables, a ceiling fan and a soda machine. No one seems to know how the place got its name. Some say it used to be a Korean Bar. Others say it was a funeral home. But all seem to agree that it has a lousy name for a pool hall. At one point, someone circulated a petition requesting the name be changed, but Mr. Kong, the proud owner, wouldn't budge. He said his pool hall would always be called the Lemon Tree Billiards House.

Mr. Kong keeps his rates very reasonable. For two dollars an hour, you can hit all of the balls you want. One day, I was in there playing eight-ball[2] with a 68-year-old parking attendant. The guy played pretty well—I was squeezing for a while—but he missed a tough slice and left me enough openings to clear the table and sink the eight-ball. I won twenty bucks.

Another guy walked up to me. He had a moustache, baseball cap and a flannel shirt.

"My name Hamilton," he said. "I ain't too good—but what—you like play?"

I ain't too good. *Sure.*

"My name's Mitch," I said. "Let's play."

We agreed on fifty bucks. Hamilton racked the balls. I broke. It was a good one. The sound of the balls cracking against each other was like a hundred glass jars exploding.

As three striped balls—the nine, twelve, and fifteen—shot into three different pockets, I noticed a goodlooking girl in a black dress sitting on a stool in the corner. I don't know if I was imagining it or not but I thought I caught her looking my way. I missed an easy shot on the side pocket. I'd burned my finger cooking *saimin*[3] and couldn't get a good grip on the cue stick.

---

[2] eight-ball—game in which players, using the plain white cue ball, must sink, or pocket, all the plain or striped balls before being allowed to sink the eight ball and win the game.

[3] *saimin*—(Hawaiian) a ramen-like noodle soup.

"Oh, too bad," said Hamilton. "Hard luck! I tot you had me deah . . ." He was what I call "a talker." The kind of guy who can't keep his mouth shut. The kind of guy who treats a game of pool like a radio call-in show.

Anyway, Hamilton hit four balls in but stalled on the fifth. I eventually won the game.

Afterwards, the girl in the black dress walked up to me.

"Hi," she said, smiling.

"Hello," I said.

"You're pretty good," she said.

"Thanks."

"You wanna play my dad?"

"Who's your dad?"

"You wanna play or not?"

"Who is he?"

"He'll give you five hundred bucks if you beat him . . ."

"Let's go."

I'm a pool hustler and the Lemon Tree Billiards House is my **turf**.[4] You see, I've been playing pool all my life. It's the only thing I know how to do. My dad taught me the game before they threw him in jail. I dropped out of school, left home, and traveled around the country challenging other pool players. I've played the best. Now I'm home.

All right, all right. I'm not a pool hustler. I'm a freshman at the University of Hawaii. And my dad's not in jail. He's an accountant. And I never challenged players around the country. I did play a game in Waipahu[5] once.

I have been playing pool for awhile, though. Sometimes I do real well. Sometimes, I don't. That's how the game is for me. Four things can happen when I pick up a cue stick. One, sometimes I feel like I'll win and I win. Two, sometimes I feel like I'll win and I lose. Three, sometimes, I feel like I'll lose and I'll lose. Four, sometimes I feel like I'll lose and I win.

---

[4] **turf**—territory.

[5] Waipahu—a town on the Hawaiian island of Oahu.

I'll tell you one thing, though. I could've been a better pool player if I hadn't been cursed. Yes, cursed.

It all happened back when I was seven years old. My dad had taken me to a beach house. I'm not sure where it was. Somewhere near Malaekahana,[6] maybe. I remember walking along the beach and seeing some large boulders. I began climbing on the rocks, trying to get a good look at the ocean and the crashing waves. The view was stunning. The water was so blue. And off shore, I thought I spotted some whales playing in the surf.

All of a sudden, my father came running down the beach. "Mitch!" he said. "Get off da rocks! Da rocks sacred! No climb up deah! No good!"

Ever since that day, I've lived with a curse. One day in the eighth grade, I dropped a touchdown pass and we lost a big intramural football game. I smashed my first car three minutes after I drove it off the lot. My first girl-friend left me for a guy in prison she read about in the papers. I'm the kind of guy who will throw down four queens in a poker game, only to watch helplessly as some clown tosses down four kings. If I buy something at the market, it'll go on sale the next day.

It hasn't been easy. The only thing I do okay is play eight-ball. But I could've been better. If it just weren't for this curse.

I don't know why I agreed to play pool with this strange girl's father. Maybe it was because she was so beautiful. The best looking woman I've ever seen. Six feet, two hundred pounds, hairy legs, moustache. Okay. Okay. So she wasn't *that* beautiful. Let's just say she was kind of average.

Anyway, we got into her car and she drove towards the Waianae coast.[7] She had one of those big, black

---

6 Malaekahana—a beach area in northern Oahu.

7 Waianae coast—western coast of Oahu.

The Lemon Tree Billiards House   151

Cadillacs you saw in the seventies. The kind Jack Lord[8] used to drive to Iolani Palace. In about a half hour or so, we wound up at a large beach house with watermills and bronze buddhas in the yard. Everywhere you looked, you saw trees. Mango, avocado, papaya, banana.

"My dad likes to plant things," the girl explained.

We walked past a rock garden and a *koi*[9] pond and she led me into a room with a pool table. There were dozens of cues lined up neatly on the wall, just like at the Lemon Tree Billiards House.

"You can grab a stick," the girl said. "I'll go get my dad."

In a few minutes, I realized why she didn't want to tell me who her father was. I was standing face to face with Locust Cordero. *The* Locust Cordero. All 6–5, 265 pounds of him. Wearing of all things, a purple tuxedo and a red carnation in his lapel. Locust Cordero, who stood trial for the murder-for-hire deaths of three Salt Lake gamblers several years back. I was about to play eight-ball with a hitman.

"Howzit," he said. "Mahalos[10] fo coming. My name Locust."

What should I say? I know who you are? I've heard of you? I've seen your mug shots on T.V.? Congratulations on your recent **acquittal**?[11] Nice tuxedo?

"Nice to meet you, sir," I said, settling on the conservative. "I'm Mitch."

We shook hands. He wore a huge jade ring on his finger.

"My daughter says you pretty good . . ."

"I try, sir."

---

[8] Jack Lord—an actor and producer best known for his role in *Hawaii Five-O*, a television series filmed in Hawaii in the sixties and seventies.

[9] *koi*—(Japanese) carp, a decorative fish.

[10] Mahalos—(Hawaiian) Thanks.

[11] **acquittal**—exoneration; setting free from a charge.

"How you like my tuxedo?" he said.

"Nice," I said.

"Shaka,[12] ah?" he said, running his hands over the material. "Silk, brah.[13] Jus bought 'em. What size you?"

"What?"

"What size you?" he repeated, opening up a closet. I was stunned. There must have been two dozen tuxedos in there. All sizes. All colors. Black, white, maroon, blue, red, pink. "Heah," said Locust, handing me a gold one. "Try put dis beauty on . . ."

"Uh," I said. "How about the black one?"

Again, I was leaning towards the conservative.

"Whatevahs," said Locust, shrugging.

I changed in the bathroom. It took me a while because I'd never worn a tuxedo before. When I walked out, Locust smiled.

"Sharp," he said. "Look at us. Now we really look like pool players . . ."

Locust chalked his cue stick. He was so big, the stick looked like a tooth pick in his hands.

"Break 'em, Mitch."

"Yes, sir."

I walked to the table and broke. I did it real fast. I don't like to think about my shots too long. That always messes me up. *Crack!* Not bad. Two solid balls shot into the right corner pocket.

"Das too bad," said Locust, shaking his head.

"Why's that, sir?" I asked.

"Cause," said Locust. "I hate to lose."

One day, not too long before, I'd visited an exorcist.[14] To get rid of my curse. He was an old Hawaiian man in his late forties or early fifties, recommended to me by a

---

[12] Shaka—Hawaiian slang referring to a hand gesture that means "Hang loose," "How's it going?" or, in this case, perhaps, "Not bad."

[13] brah—brother; like "bro."

[14] exorcist—individual who gets rid of an evil spirit using objects, ritualistic incantations, and other methods.

friend. When I called for an appointment, he said he couldn't fit me in. There were a lot of folks out there with problems, I guessed. I told him it was an emergency.

"Okay, come ovah," he said. "But hurry up."

I drove to his house. He lived in Palolo Valley. I was very scared. What would happen? I could see it now. As soon as I walked into the room, the man would scream and run away from me. He'd tell me he saw death and destruction written all over my face. The wind would blow papers all over his room and I'd be speaking weird languages I had never heard before and blood and mucous would pour out my mouth.

But nothing like that happened. I walked into his house, expecting to see him chanting or praying. Instead, he was sitting behind a *koa*[15] desk in a Munsingwear shirt and green polyester pants.

"Dis bettah be good," he said. "I went cancel my tee time at da Ala Wai fo you. . ."

I smiled. I told him my **plight**.[16] I started from the beginning—telling him about the day I climbed on the rocks and the bad luck I've had ever since.

"You ain't cursed," the man said. He bent down to pick something up from the floor. What was it? An ancient amulet? A charm? None of the above. It was a golf club. An eight iron. "Da mind is one very powerful ting," he said, waving the right iron around like a magician waving a wand. "It can make simple tings difficult and difficult tings simple."

"What about the rocks?" I said.

"Tink positive," the man said. "You one negative buggah. Da only curse is in yo mind."

That's it? No reading scripture. No chanting?

"I tell you one ting, brah," the Hawaiian man said. "One day, you going encountah one challenge. If you

---

[15] *koa*—(Hawaiian) rare furniture wood from a species of acacia tree.

[16] **plight**—predicament; problem.

beat em, da curse going to *pau*.[17] But, if you lose, da rest of yo life going shrivel up like one slug aftah you pour salt on top . . ."

"Anything else?" I said.

"Yeah," said the Hawaiian man. "You owe me twenty bucks."

Locust and I had played ten games. We'd agreed on eleven. I'd won five, he'd won five. In between, his daughter brought us fruit punch and smoked marlin.[18] It was already dark. I had an Oceanography test the next day.

On the final game, I hit an incredible shot—the cue ball jumping over Locust's ball like a fullback leaping over a tackler and hitting the seven into the side pocket. This seemed to piss Locust off. He came right back with a beauty of his own—a masse I couldn't believe. In a masse, the cue ball does bizarre things on the table after being hit—like weaving between balls as if it has a mind of its own. Those are the trick shots you see on T.V. Anyway, Locust hit a masse, where the cue ball hit not one, not two, not three, but four of his balls into four different holes. *Come on!* I was convinced Locust could make the cue ball spell his name across the green velvet sky of the pool table.

Pretty soon, it was just me, Locust, and the eight ball. I looked at Locust, real fast, and he stared at me like a starving man sizing up a Diner's chicken *katsu*[19] plate lunch. I took a shot but my arm felt like a lead pipe and I missed everything. Locust took a deep breath, blew his shot, and swore in three different languages. It was my turn.

And then I realized it. This was the moment that would make or break me. The challenge the exorcist guy was talking about. I had to win.

---

[17] *pau*—(Hawaiian) end; finish.

[18] marlin—large oceanic sport fish.

[19] *katsu*—(Japanese) breaded and deep-fried cutlet.

I measured the table, paused, and said the words that would change my life and save me from shrivelling up like a slug with salt poured on it.

"Eight ball. Corner pocket."

I would have to be careful. Gentle. It was a tough slice to the right corner pocket. If I hit the cue ball too hard, it could fall into the wrong pocket. That would be a scratch. I would lose.

I took a deep breath, cocked my stick, and aimed. I hit the cue ball softly. From here, everything seemed to move in slow motion. The cue ball tapped the eight ball and the eight ball seemed to take hours to roll towards the hole. Out of the corner of my eye, I saw Locust's daughter standing up from her seat, her hands covering her mouth.

Clack. *Plop.*

The ball fell into the hole. The curse was lifted. I had won. I would have been a happy man if I hadn't been so scared.

Locust walked up to me, shaking his head. He reached into his pocket. Oh, no. Here it comes. He was gonna take out his gun, shoot me, and bury my body at some deserted beach. Goodbye, cruel world. Thanks for the memories . . .

"I no can remembah da last time I wen lose," he said, pulling out his wallet and handing me five crispy one hundred dollar bills. "Mahalos fo da game."

Locust asked me to stay and talk for awhile. We sat on straw chairs next to the pool table. The place was dark except for several gas-lit torches, hissing like leaky tires. Hanging on the walls were fishing nets and dried, preserved fish, lobsters, and turtles.

"You must be wond'ring why we wearing dese tuxedos," said Locust.

"Yeah," I said.

"Well, dis whole night, it's kinda one big deal fo me." Locust leaned towards me. "You see, brah, I nevah leave my house in five years . . ."

"Why?" I said. I couldn't believe it.

"All my life, evry'body been scared of me," said Locust, sighing. "Ev'rywheah I go, people look at me funny. Dey whispah behind my back . . ."

"But . . ."

"Lemme tell you someting," he continued. "Dey went try me fo murder coupla times. Both times, da jury said I was innocent. Still, people no like Locust around. Dey no like see me. And das why, I never step foot outta dis place."

"Forgive me for saying so, sir," I said. "But that's kinda sad. That's no way to live . . ."

"Oh, it ain't dat bad," said Locust. "I play pool. I go in da ocean, spear *uhu*.[20] I trow net fo mullet. Once in a while, I go in da mountains behind da house and shoot one pig . . ."

"But don't you ever miss getting out and walking around the city. Experiencing life?"

I was getting nervous again. I mean, here I was, giving advice on how to live to Locust Cordero. After I had just beaten the guy at eight-ball.

"Whasso great about walking around da streets of da city?" said Locust, after awhile. "People shooting and stabbing each othah. Talking stink about each othah. Stealing each othah's husbands and wives. Breaking each othah's hearts . . ."

"You scared?" I said, pressing my luck.

"Yeah," said Locust, looking me straight in the eye. "I guess I am."

We didn't say anything for awhile. I could hear the waves of the ocean breaking on the beach.

---

[20] *uhu*—(Hawaiian) parrot fish.

"So," said Locust, shifting in his seat. "Where you went learn fo shoot pool?"

"The Lemon Tree Billiards House," I said.

"Da Lemon Tree Billards House?" Locust said, shaking his head. "What kine name dat? Sound like one funeral home . . ."

"Sir," I said. "I'm sorry. Can I say something?"

"Sure."

"You're living your life like a prisoner. You might as well have been convicted of murder and locked in jail."

Yeah, sometimes it seems I just don't know when to shut up.

"Evah since I was one kid, I had hard luck," said Locust, moving closer to me and whispering. "You see, I'm cursed . . ."

"You're what?" I said, surprised.

"I'm cursed," Locust repeated, raising his voice. "Jeez, fo one young kid, you got lousy hearing, ah? Must be all dat loud music you buggahs listen to nowadays."

"How'd you get cursed?" I said.

"One day, when I was one kid, I was climbing some rocks looking out at da ocean. Down Malaekahana side. All of a sudden, my bruddah start screaming, 'Get down from deah. No good. Da rocks sacred. '"

I couldn't believe it. Locust and I were cursed by the same rocks. We were curse brothers.

"Da ting's beat me," said Locust, shaking his head.

"You're talking like a loser."

"A what?" said Locust, getting out of his chair.

"Locust," I said, my voice cracking. "I lived with the same curse and I beat it . . ."

"How?" said Locust, sitting back down. "I tried everything. Hawaiian salt. Ti[21] leaves. Da works . . ."

"You gotta believe in yourself."

---

[21] *Ti*—(Hawaiian) tropical plant.

"How you do dat?"

"With your mind," I said. "See, the first thing you gotta do is meet a challenge and beat it," I said. "Go outside. Walk the streets. Meet people . . ."

"You evah stop fo tink how dangerous da world is?" said Locust. "Tink about it. How many things out deah are ready, waiting, fo screw you up. Death, sickness, corruption, greed, old age . . ."

It was scary. Locust was starting to make sense.

"I don't know," I finally said.

"Tink about it," said Locust. "Tink about it."

One day, several weeks later, I was playing eight-ball at the Lemon Tree Billiards House. Several people were arguing about the source of an unusual smell. Some said it came from a cardboard box filled with rotten *choy sum*[22] outside on the sidewalk in front of the pool hall. Others said it was Kona winds[23] blowing in the pungent smell of *taegu*[24] from Yuni's Bar B-Q. Still others said the peculiar smell came from Old Man Rivera, who sat in a corner eating a lunch he had made at home. Too much *patis*—fish sauce—in his *sari sari*.[25]

"If you like good smell," said Mr. Kong, the owner of the Lemon Tree Billiards House. "Go orchid farm. If you like play pool, come da Lemon Tree Billiards House."

I was on table number three with a young Japanese guy with short hair. He had dark glasses and wore a black suit. He looked like he was in the *yakuza*.[26]

I had already beaten three guys. I was on a roll. It gets like that every now and then. When you know you can't miss.

The Yakuza guy never smiled. And everytime he missed a shot, he swore at himself. Pretty soon, he started

---

[22] *choy sum*—(Chinese) flowering cabbage.

[23] Kona winds—winds from the west coast of the island of Hawaii.

[24] *taegu*—seasoned dried codfish or cuttlefish.

[25] *sari sari*—food.

[26] *yakuza*—(Japanese) criminal organization.

to hit the balls very hard—thrusting his cue stick like a samurai spearing an opponent. He was off, though, and I eventually won the game.

"You saw how I beat the *Yakuza* guy?" I said to Mr. Kong, who was now on a stepladder unscrewing a burned-out lightbulb.

"*Yakuza* guy?" said Mr. Kong. "What *yakuza* guy?"

"The Japanese guy in the suit . . ." I said.

"Oh," said Mr. Kong, laughing like crazy. "You talking about Yatsu! Das my neighbor. He ain't no *yakuza*. He one pre-school teachah . . ."

Just then, Locust Cordero walked into the Lemon Tree Billiards House. Mr. Kong stopped laughing. Everyone stopped their games. No one said a word. The only sound you heard was the ticking of a clock on the wall.

"Mitch," said Locust. "I went take yo advice. I no like live like one prisonah no moah . . ."

I was speechless.

"You know what dey say," said Locust. "Feel like one five hundred pound bait lifted from my shoulders . . ."

"Weight," I said.

"Fo what?" said Locust, obviously confused.

"No, no," I said. "Five hundred pound *weight*. Not bait . . ."

"Whatevahs," said Locust. "Da curse is gone . . ."

He walked over to Mr. Kong's finest tables, ran his thick fingers over the smooth wood, and looked into the deep pockets like a child staring down a mysterious well.

"Eight-ball?" he asked, turning to me.

"Yeah," I said, smiling. "Yeah, sure."

QUESTIONS TO CONSIDER

1. What, in your opinion, makes Mitch such a likable character?

2. Why do you think Mitch first says he's a pool hustler and then immediately changes his story to the truth?

3. What does the "curse" represent?

4. How were Mitch and Locust each the victim of stereotypes and belief systems that held them prisoner?

5. What does the story as a whole have to say about appearances and realities—and getting to know someone different from you?

Balancing
Two Worlds

Chapter 4

On Being Asian American

BY LAWSON FUSAO INADA

*Lawson Fusao Inada (1938–   ), a Sansei, or third-generation
Japanese American, was born in California. During World War II, he
and his family were interned in camps in Arkansas and Colorado.
Out of that experience came* Before the War: Poems as They
Happened *(1971), the first volume of poems by a Japanese
American published by a major American publisher. Later volumes
include* Legends from Camp *(1993) and* Drawing the Line.
*Inada's poems have inspired a symphony and been carved in stone
along a river in Oregon. In this poem from* Legends from Camp,
*Inada acknowledges the difficulties of being an Asian American but
expresses pride in his dual heritage.*

for Our Children
Of course, not everyone
can be an Asian American.
Distinctions are earned,
and deserve dedication.

Thus, from time of birth,
the journey awaits you—
ventures through time,
the turns of the earth.

When you seem to arrive,
the journey continues;
when you seem to arrive,
the journey continues.

Take me as I am, you cry,
I, I, am an individual.
Which certainly is true.
Which generates an echo.

Who are all your people
assembled in celebration,
with wisdom and strength,
to which you are entitled.

For you are at the head
of succeeding generations[1]
as the rest of the world
comes forward to greet you.

---

[1] succeeding generations—generations to come.

QUESTIONS TO CONSIDER

1. Who do you think is the audience for Inada's poem?

2. How would you explain the feeling of the third stanza, and what does Inada want to convey?

3. What effect does italicizing the last two lines of each stanza have on the reader?

4. How does Inada see the struggle between wanting to be seen as an individual and being a part of a group with a long history?

5. With what spirit does Inada try to convince his audience to balance two worlds?

from

The Woman Warrior

BY MAXINE HONG KINGSTON

Maxine Hong Kingston, born in 1940 in Stockton, California, has published several books that focus on her Chinese heritage. She wrote China Men, Tripmaster Monkey: His Fake Book, *and* The Woman Warrior: Memoirs of a Girlhood Among Ghosts *(1975), which won the National Book Critics Circle Award for nonfiction. In the following selection, the narrator bemoans the expectations that Chinese villagers had for girls and describes how they affected her upbringing in the United States. She tells her story as a form of revenge.*

My American life has been such a disappointment.

"I got straight A's, Mama."

"Let me tell you a true story about a girl who saved her village."

I could not figure out what was my village. And it was important that I do something big and fine, or else my parents would sell me when we made our way back to China. In China there were solutions for what to do with little girls who ate up food and threw tantrums. You can't eat straight A's.

When one of my parents or the emigrant villagers[1] said, "'Feeding girls is feeding cowbirds,'" I would thrash on the floor and scream so hard I couldn't talk. I couldn't stop.

"What's the matter with her?"

"l don't know. Bad, I guess. You know how girls are. 'There's no profit in raising girls. Better to raise geese than girls.'"

"l would hit her if she were mine. But then there's no use wasting all that discipline on a girl. 'When you raise girls, you're raising children for strangers.'"

"Stop that crying!" my mother would yell. "I'm going to hit you if you don't stop. Bad girl! Stop!" I'm going to remember never to hit or to scold my children for crying, I thought, because then they will only cry more.

"I'm not a bad girl," I would scream. "I'm not a bad girl. I'm not a bad girl." I might as well have said, "I'm not a girl."

"When you were little, all you had to say was 'I'm not a bad girl,' and you could make yourself cry," my mother says, talking-story[2] about my childhood.

I minded that the emigrant villagers shook their heads at my sister and me. "One girl—and another girl," they said, and made our parents ashamed to take us out together. The good part about my brothers being born was that people stopped saying, "All girls," but I learned new **grievances**.[3] "Did you roll an egg on *my* face like that when *I* was born?" "Did you have a full-month party for *me*?" "Did you turn on all the lights?"

---

[1] emigrant villagers—immigrants who live nearby but who retain traditional Chinese beliefs.

[2] talking-story—telling an anecdote.

[3] **grievances**—circumstances seen as just causes for protest.

"Did you send *my* picture to Grandmother?"[4] "Why not? Because I'm a girl? Is that why not?" "Why didn't you teach me English?" "You like having me beaten up at school, don't you?"

"She is very mean, isn't she?" the emigrant villagers would say.

"Come, children. Hurry. Hurry. Who wants to go out with Great-Uncle?" On Saturday mornings my great-uncle, the ex-river pirate, did the shopping. "Get your coats, whoever's coming."

"I'm coming. I'm coming. Wait for me."

When he heard girls' voices, he turned on us and roared, "No girls!" and left my sisters and me hanging our coats back up, not looking at one another. The boys came back with candy and new toys. When they walked through Chinatown, the people must have said, "A boy—and another boy—and another boy!" At my great-uncle's funeral I secretly tested out feeling glad that he was dead—the six-foot bearish masculinity of him.

I went away to college—Berkeley in the sixties—and I studied, and I marched to change the world, but I did not turn into a boy. I would have liked to bring myself back as a boy for my parents to welcome with chickens and pigs. That was for my brother, who returned alive from Vietnam.

If I went to Vietnam, I would not come back; females desert families. It was said, "There is an outward tendency in females," which meant that I was getting straight A's for the good of my future husband's family, not my own. I did not plan ever to have a husband. I would show my mother and father and the nosey emigrant villagers that girls have no outward tendency. I stopped getting straight A's.

And all the time I was having to turn myself American-feminine, or no dates.

---

[4] These are four acts that celebrate the valued birth of a son.

There is a Chinese word for the female *I*—which is "slave." Break the women with their own tongues!

I refused to cook. When I had to wash dishes, I would crack one or two. "Bad girl," my mother yelled, and sometimes that made me **gloat**[5] rather than cry. Isn't a bad girl almost a boy?

"What do you want to be when you grow up, little girl?"

"A lumberjack in Oregon." . . .

I live now where there are Chinese and Japanese, but no emigrants from my own village looking at me as if I had failed them. Living among one's own emigrant villagers can give a good Chinese far from China glory and a place. "That old busboy is really a swordsman," we whisper when he goes by, "He's a swordsman who's killed fifty. He has a tong[6] ax in his closet." But I am useless, one more girl who couldn't be sold. When I visit the family now, I wrap my American successes around me like a private shawl; I *am* worthy of eating the food. From afar I can believe my family loves me **fundamentally**.[7] They only say, "When fishing for treasures in the flood, be careful not to pull in girls," because that is what one says about daughters. But I watched such words come out of my own mother's and father's mouths; I looked at their ink drawing of poor people snagging their neighbors' **flotage**[8] with long flood hooks and pushing the girl babies on down the river. And I had to get out of hating range. I read in an anthropology book that Chinese say, "Girls are necessary too"; I have never heard the Chinese I know make this **concession**.[9] Perhaps it was a saying in

---

[5] **gloat**—think about something with great, triumphant satisfaction.

[6] **tong**—belonging to a member of a tong (an association, or, earlier, a secret society).

[7] **fundamentally**—basically; essentially.

[8] **flotage**—floating objects.

[9] **concession**—reluctant acknowledgement.

another village. I refuse to shy my way[10] anymore through our Chinatown, which tasks me[11] with the old sayings and the stories.

The swordswoman[12] and I are not so dissimilar. May my people understand the resemblance soon so that I can return to them. What we have in common are the words at our backs. The **idioms**[13] for *revenge* are "report a crime" and "report to five families." The reporting is the vengeance—not the beheading, not the gutting, but the words. And I have so many words—"chink" words and "gook" words too—that they do not fit on my skin.

---

[10] shy my way—walk shyly and modestly.

[11] tasks me—censures or reproaches; a variation of the phrase "to take to task."

[12] swordswoman—the legendary "woman warrior" of the book title, *Fa Mu Lan.*

[13] **idioms**—expressions that have a particular meaning that can't be understood from the individual words.

QUESTIONS TO CONSIDER

1. How does the narrator feel about being female?

2. In what ways does she choose to make her feelings known?

3. How successfully does the narrator reconcile her identity as both Chinese and American?

4. What is the narrator saying in the last paragraph? What other words does she have than the ones she lists? How is she using her words?

Lost Sister

BY CATHY SONG

Cathy Song (1955–   ) was born in Hawaii to a Korean father who had come to Hawaii with the first group of Korean laborers and a Chinese-American mother who was a "picture bride." The family traveled often, and Song started writing by recording anec-dotes contributed by everyone in her family. Her poems have appeared in many literary journals, and her first volume of poetry, Picture Bride (1983), won the prestigious Yale Series of Younger Poets award. In this poem, Song contrasts the lives of two sisters and suggests that heritage is just as important as nationality.

In China,
even the peasants
named their first daughters
Jade—
the stone that in the far fields
could moisten the dry season,
could make men move mountains
for the healing green of the inner hills
glistening like slices of winter melon.

And the daughters were grateful:
They never left home.
To move freely was a luxury
stolen from them at birth.
Instead, they gathered patience,
learning to walk in shoes
the size of teacups,[1]
without breaking—
the arc of their movements
as **dormant**[2] as the rooted willow,
as **redundant**[3] as the farmyard hens.
But they traveled far
in surviving,
learning to stretch the family rice,
to quiet the demons,
the noisy stomachs.

---

[1] The image refers to the old Chinese practice of binding upper-class women's feet. A footprint of 2" or 3" in length was deemed ideal.

[2] **dormant**—inactive; asleep.

[3] **redundant**—excessive; superfluous.

II

There is a sister
across the ocean,
who **relinquished**[4] her name,
diluting jade green
with the blue of the Pacific.
Rising with a tide of locusts,
she swarmed with others
to **inundate**[5] another shore.
In America,
there are many roads
and women can stride along with men.

But in another wilderness,
the possibilities,
the loneliness,
can strangulate like jungle vines.
The meager provisions and sentiments
of once belonging—
fermented roots, Mah Jong[6] tiles and
    firecrackers—set but
a flimsy household
in a forest of nightless cities.
A giant snake rattles above,
spewing black clouds into your kitchen.
Dough-faced landlords
slip in and out of your keyholes,
making claims you don't understand,
tapping into your communication systems
of laundry lines and restaurant chains.

---

[4] **relinquished**—gave up.

[5] **inundate**—flood.

[6] Mah Jong—a Chinese game.

You find you need China:
your one fragile identification,
a jade link
handcuffed to your wrist.
You remember your mother
who walked for centuries,
footless—
and like her,
you have left no footprints,
but only because
there is an ocean in between,
the **unremitting**[7] space of your rebellion.

---

[7] **unremitting**—constant; endless.

QUESTIONS TO CONSIDER

1. Why does Song divide her poem into two sections?

2. What is the significance of the girl's name Jade and why would such girls be grateful to be so named?

3. How does Song describe the sister in the first part of the poem, and why do you think she respects her travels?

4. How does Song describe the "wilderness" in which immigrants in America wander? Why is it such a difficult land to cross?

5. What can you learn from this poem about how Song has tried to balance her two worlds?

Mother Tongue

BY AMY TAN

Born in 1952 in Oakland, California, Amy Tan grew up in the California towns of Fresno and Berkeley. Her father had emigrated from China in 1947; her mother, in 1949. Tan worked as a freelance technical writer before publishing her first novel, The Joy Luck Club. *She has published two other novels—The Kitchen God's Wife and* The Hundred Secret Senses—*and two children's books:* The Moon Lady *and* The Chinese Siamese Cat. *"Mother Tongue" was included in* The Best American Essays *(1991). In it, Tan argues that because her mother's spoken language "helped shape the way I saw things, expressed things, made sense of the world," it should not be labeled 'broken English.'*

I am not a scholar of English or literature. I cannot give you much more than personal opinions on the English language and its variations in this country or others.

I am a writer. And by that definition, I am someone who has always loved language. I am fascinated by language in daily life. I spend a great deal of my time thinking about the power of language—the way it can **evoke**[1] an emotion, a visual image, a complex idea, or a simple truth. Language is the tool of my trade. And I use them all—all the Englishes I grew up with.

Recently, I was made keenly aware of the different Englishes I do use. I was giving a talk to a large group of people, the same talk I had already given to half a dozen other groups. The nature of the talk was about my writing, my life, and my book, *The Joy Luck Club*. The talk was going along well enough, until I remembered one major difference that made the whole talk sound wrong. My mother was in the room. And it was perhaps the first time she had heard me give a lengthy speech, using the kind of English I have never used with her. I was saying things like, "The intersection of memory upon imagination" and "There is an aspect of my fiction that relates to thus-and-thus"— a speech filled with carefully wrought grammatical phrases, burdened, it suddenly seemed to me, with nominalized forms, past perfect tenses, conditional phrases, all the forms of standard English that I had learned in school and through books, the forms of English I did not use at home with my mother.

Just last week, I was walking down the street with my mother, and I again found myself conscious of the English I was using, the English I do use with her. We were talking about the price of new and used furniture and I heard myself saying this: "Not waste money that way." My husband was with us as well, and he didn't notice any switch in my English. And then I realized why. It's because over the twenty years we've been together I've often used that same kind of English with him, and sometimes he even uses it with me. It has become our language of intimacy, a different sort of English that relates to family talk, the language I grew up with.

---

[1] **evoke**—call forth.

So you'll have some idea of what this family talk I heard sounds like, I'll quote what my mother said during a recent conversation which I videotaped and then transcribed. During this conversation, my mother was talking about a political gangster in Shang-hai who had the same last name as her family's, Du, and how the gangster in his early years wanted to be adopted by her family, which was rich by comparison. Later, the gangster became more powerful, far richer than my mother's family, and one day showed up at my mother's wedding to pay his respects. Here's what she said in part:

"Du Yusong having business like fruit stand. Like off the street kind. He is Du like Du Zong—but not Tsung-ming Island people. The local people call putong, the river east side, he belong to that side local people. That man want to ask Du Zong father take him in like become own family. Du Zong father wasn't look down on him, but didn't take seriously, until that man big like become a mafia. Now important person, very hard to inviting him. Chinese way, came only to show respect, don't stay for dinner. Respect for making big celebration, he shows up. Mean gives lots of respect. Chinese custom. Chinese social life that way. If too important won't have to stay too long. He come to my wedding. I didn't see, I heard it. I gone to boy's side, they have YMCA dinner. Chinese age I was nineteen."

You should know that my mother's expressive command of English **belies**[2] how much she actually understands. She reads the *Forbes* report, listens to *Wall Street Week*, converses daily with her stockbroker, reads all of Shirley MacLaine's books with ease—all kinds of things I can't begin to understand. Yet some of my friends tell me they understand 50 percent of what my mother says. Some say they understand 80 to 90 percent. Some say they understand none of it as if she were

---

[2] **belies**—camouflages; misrepresents.

speaking pure Chinese. But to me, my mother's English is perfectly clear, perfectly natural. It's my mother tongue. Her language, as I hear it, is vivid, direct, full of observation and imagery. That was the language that helped shape the way I saw things, expressed things, made sense of the world.

Lately, I've been giving more thought to the kind of English my mother speaks. Like others, I have described it to people as "broken" or "fractured" English. But I **wince**[3] when I say that. It has always bothered me that I can think of no way to describe it other than "broken," as if it were damaged and needed to be fixed, as if it lacked a certain wholeness and soundness. I've heard other terms used, "limited English," for example. But they seem just as bad, as if everything is limited, including people's perceptions of the limited English speaker.

I know this for a fact, because when I was growing up, my mother's "limited" English limited *my* perception of her. I was ashamed of her English. I believed that her English reflected the quality of what she had to say. That is, because she expressed them imperfectly, her thoughts were imperfect. And I had plenty of **empirical**[4] evidence to support me: the fact that people in department stores, at banks, and at restaurants did not take her seriously, did not give her good service, pretended not to understand her, or even acted as if they did not hear her.

My mother has long realized the limitations of her English as well. When I was fifteen, she used to have me call people on the phone to pretend I was she. In this **guise**,[5] I was forced to ask for information or even to complain and yell at people who had been rude to her. One time it was a call to her stockbroker in New York. She had cashed out her small portfolio and it just so happened

---

[3] **wince**—a shrinking or startled movement.
[4] **empirical**—gained from observation.
[5] **guise**—false appearance.

we were going to go to New York the next week, our very first trip outside California. I had to get on the phone and say in an adolescent voice that was not very convincing, "This is Mrs. Tan."

And my mother was standing in the back whispering loudly, "Why he don't send me check, already two weeks late. So mad he lie to me, losing me money."

And then I said in perfect English, "Yes, I'm getting rather concerned. You had agreed to send the check two weeks ago, but it hasn't arrived."

Then she began to talk more loudly. "What he want. I come to New York tell him front of his boss, you cheating me?" And I was trying to calm her down, make her be quiet, while telling the stockbroker, "I can't tolerate any more excuses. If I don't receive the check immediately, I am going to have to speak to your manager when I'm in New York next week." And sure enough, the following week there we were in front of this astonished stockbroker, and I was sitting there red-faced and quiet, and my mother, the real Mrs. Tan, was shouting at his boss in her **impeccable**[6] broken English.

We used a similar routine just five days ago, for a situation that was far less humorous. My mother had gone to the hospital for an appointment, to find out about a benign brain tumor a CAT scan had revealed a month ago. She said she had spoken very good English, her best English, no mistakes. Still, she said, the hospital did not apologize when they said they had lost the CAT scan and she had come for nothing. She said they did not seem to have any sympathy when she told them she was anxious to know the exact diagnosis, since her husband and son had both died of brain tumors. She said they would not give her any more information until the next time and she would have to make another appointment for that. So she said she would not leave until the doctor called her

---

[6] **impeccable**—faultless.

daughter. She wouldn't budge. And when the doctor finally called her daughter, me, who spoke in perfect English—lo and behold—we had assurances that CAT scan would be found, promises that a conference call on Monday would be held, and apologies for any suffering my mother had gone through for a most regrettable mistake.

I think my mother's English almost had an effect on limiting my possibilities in life as well. Sociologists and linguists probably will tell you that a person's developing language skills are more influenced by peers. But I do think that the language spoken in the family, especially in immigrant families which are more **insular**,[7] plays a large role in shaping the language of the child. And I believe that it affected my results on achievement tests, IQ tests, and the SAT. While my English skills were never judged as poor, compared to math, English could not be considered my strong suit. In grade school I did moderately well, getting perhaps B's, sometimes B-pluses, in English and scoring perhaps in the sixtieth or seventieth percentile on achievement tests. But those scores were not good enough to override the opinion that my true abilities lay in math and science, because in those areas I achieved A's and scored in the ninetieth percentile or higher.

This was understandable. Math is precise: there is only one correct answer. Whereas, for me at least, the answers on English tests were always a judgment call, a matter of opinion and personal experience. Those tests were constructed around items like fill-in-the-blank sentence completion, such as, "Even though Tom was _____ , Mary thought he was _____ ." And the correct answer always seemed to be the most bland combinations of thoughts, for example, "Even though Tom was shy, Mary thought he was charming," with the grammatical structure "even though" limiting the

---

[7] **insular**—narrow; provincial.

correct answer to some sort of semantic opposites, so you wouldn't get answers like, "Even though Tom was foolish, Mary thought he was ridiculous." Well, according to my mother, there were very few limitations as to what Tom could have been and what Mary might have thought of him. So I never did well on tests like that.

The same was true with word analogies, pairs of words in which you were supposed to find some sort of logical-semantic relationship—for example, "*Sunset* is to *nightfall* as _____ is to _____." And here you would be presented with a list of four possible pairs, one of which showed the same kind of relationship: *red* is to *stoplight, bus* is to *arrival, chills* is to *fever, yawns* is to *boring*. Well, I could never think that way. I knew what the tests were asking, but I could not block out of my mind the images already created by the first pair, "*sunset* is to *nightfall*"—and I would see a burst of colors against a darkening sky, the moon rising, the lowering of a curtain of stars. And all the other pairs of words—red, bus, stoplight, boring—just threw up a mass of confusing images, making it impossible for me to sort out something as logical as saying: "A sunset precedes nightfall" is the same as "a chill precedes a fever." The only way I would have gotten that answer right would have been to imagine an associative situation, for example, my being disobedient and staying out past sunset, catching a chill at night, which turns into a feverish pneumonia as punishment, which indeed did happen to me.

I have been thinking about all this lately, about my mother's English, about achievement tests. Because lately I've been asked, as a writer, why there are not more Asian Americans represented in American literature. Why are there few Asian Americans enrolled in creative writing programs? Why do so many Chinese students go into engineering? Well, these are broad sociological questions I can't begin to answer. But I have noticed in surveys—in fact, just last week—that Asian students, as a whole, always do significantly better on math achievement tests than in English. And this makes me think that there are other Asian American students whose English spoken in the home might also be described as "broken" or "limited." And perhaps they also have teachers who are steering them away from writing and into math and science, which is what happened to me.

Fortunately, I happen to be rebellious in nature and enjoy the challenge of disproving assumptions made about me. I became an English major my first year in college, after being enrolled as pre-med. I started writing nonfiction as a freelancer the week after I was told by my former boss that writing was my worst skill and I should **hone**[8] my talents toward account management.

But it wasn't until 1985 that I finally began to write fiction. And at first I wrote using what I thought to be wittily crafted sentences, sentences that would finally prove I had mastery over the English language. Here's an example from the first draft of a story that later made its way into *The Joy Luck Club*, but without this line: "That was my mental **quandary**[9] in its **nascent**[10] state." A terrible line, which I can barely pronounce.

Fortunately, for reasons I won't get into today, I later decided I should envision a reader for the stories I would write. And the reader I decided upon was my mother, because these were stories about mothers. So with this reader in mind—and in fact she did read my early drafts—I began to write stories using all the Englishes I grew up with: the English I spoke to my mother, which for lack of a better term might be described as "simple"; the English she used with me, which for lack of a better term might be described as "broken"; my translation of her Chinese, which could

---

[8] **hone**—sharpen.
[9] **quandary**—dilemma.
[10] **nascent**—beginning.

certainly be described as "watered down"; and what I imagined to be her translation of her Chinese if she could speak in perfect English, her internal language, and for that I sought to preserve the essence, but neither an English nor a Chinese structure. I wanted to capture what language ability tests can never reveal: her intent, her passion, her imagery, the rhythms of her speech and the nature of her thoughts.

Apart from what any critic had to say about my writing, I knew I had succeeded where it counted when my mother finished reading my book and gave me her verdict: "So easy to read."

QUESTIONS TO CONSIDER

1. What two meanings does the title of this essay suggest?

2. In what ways is her inability to speak "proper" English a problem for the mother?

3. Tan analyzes why many children of immigrants have difficulty with English. Do you agree with her analysis?

4. How could Tan's essay be used as an attack on or a defense of her mother's "tongue"?

5. To what extent should immigrants be forced to learn proper English?

Those Years

BY T.C. HUO

T. C. Huo emigrated from Laos to the United States in the early 1980s. He received a master's degree in creative writing from the University of California at Irvine and, in 1998, he published a novel, A Thousand Wings. *In this story, originally published in the* Seattle Review *(1988), the narrator honors his heritage and family history as he courageously brings to light memories of family members and the life he was forced to leave behind in Laos.*

The Mekong is a river by which a villager, probably a fisherman, on one misty morning heard a baby's cry. The king's advisers, because they discovered the baby prince at the time of his birth had a set of thirty-two teeth lining in two rows and could already speak fluently, considered him evil, bound to **incur**[1] bad luck to the kingdom. They advised the king to send the baby in exile at once.

They put the baby in a basket and sent him down the river, knowing that he would be drowned or starved to death.

---

[1] **incur**—bring upon itself.

Currents carried him, sleeping, tucked in a blanket. The basket flowed and flowed. By morning it was caught in a cluster of twining bodhi[2] roots, along the river bank, where a fisherman found the baby.

The villagers revered him as a **prodigy**.[3] He grew up to be a king, established a kingdom by the river, in a land where elephants roamed.

The place became known as the Kingdom of a Million Elephants, in which I was born.

Because Grandma had forbidden me to go near the river, I didn't let her know about my trip to the pier to watch the sunset with a classmate.

We sat by the steps, drowned in the sunset that dyed the river. Merchants **disembarked**[4] from a barge, a dark outline against the shimmering surface of the water, like a goldfish's armor of scales. Sparrows, arguing and gossiping, flew in and out of the tamarind tree[5] by the steps. My classmate sighed and, hands on his knees, said I should write a poem to commit the passing moment to eternity.

About two miles from the pier was a temple, where Grandmother often took me. At the back of the temple stood a statue of Buddha, about three stories high, facing the river, presiding over it.

The Buddha loomed overhead: the oblong ears with pointed lobes, the broad forehead, the red dot between the eyebrows.

Looking up at the Buddha made me dizzy: the towering features seemed alive, seemed to sense and know. For this reason, at home I often knelt in front of the pillow and prayed, "Protect us, protect our family,

---

[2] bodhi—tall trees of the ficus family with great spreading roots. They are known as bodhi trees because, according to Buddhist tradition, Buddha sat under one when he attained enlightenment (bodhi).

[3] **prodigy**—exceptionally talented individual.

[4] **disembarked**—went ashore.

[5] tamarind tree—tropical Asian evergreen tree with a hard, yellowish wood, yellow flowers with red stripes, and edible fruit.

provide us with safety and health," and bowed three times on the pillow before going to sleep.

Looking down, I saw a steep flight of stairs arching out to the river, the brown currents rolling by. I felt dizzy and shut my eyes. On religious occasions, monks took the stairs and went down to the river to release caged clams, a gesture of releasing life, multiplying it.

I did not connect the Mekong with death even when my teacher's sister, the **valedictorian**,[6] got drowned in 1975. It happened on the first day of the Water-Splashing Festival. People crossed the river to party at the small islands in its middle. The accident happened on the way back—too many people were in the boat. Other girls were saved. Except the valedictorian. She clung too hard to the young man who tried to rescue her. Rescuing other drowning girls had worn him out. But he plunged back into the river for the last one, the valedictorian. She dragged him down.

In 1976, after the **emancipation**,[7] I crossed the river for the first time, on a field trip. It took the barge ten to fifteen minutes to cross. The motor churned the water. The ripples rolled. The pier looked diminished, the shore distant. I found myself in the center of a giant well.

The Mekong, in Laos, flows from the north through my hometown, Luang Prabang, to the capital, and separates Laos from Thailand. In the late seventies, people got drowned, got shot as they tried to escape to Thailand. Some were caught and sent back; some were robbed and then murdered. My classmate, the one who suggested I write a poem, swam across the river. His family in Laos didn't hear of him. No one in the refugee

---

[6] **valedictorian**—person with the highest rank in a graduating class.

[7] **emancipation**—In 1975, the area of Laos was united under one native government for the first time in 300 years. A communist government, it nationalized private industry and private property and rigidly controlled political and social communication. By 1979, the majority of the country's educated and skilled people had been eliminated or had fled.

camp saw him. In fact no one on either side had ever seen him again. He simply disappeared.

Maybe the Pathet Lao[8] had caught him and sent him up north for a brainwash or shot him. Who knows? More than likely he was drowned. Later on his family crossed the border. In the camp, I saw his parents and sisters, plus an absence.

I saw many absences, among them was Buddha, who presided over the Mekong and did nothing as if he did not see, did not know.

Under the pale fluorescent light in the hut, Grandmother turned away from me, looked down, and whispered, as if she were afraid that her breath would blow away the particles on the table, "Coming back? Returning? He's here." She patted my hand. "He's with us now." I had just rejoined my family in the camp.

Two praying mantes[9] crawled slowly up the bamboo pole, the smaller one following her mother. To see them, I had to follow where Grandmother was looking when she spoke.

She talked to the praying mantes, "Coming back to see us? You want to be with us? You want to—" She took out her damp handkerchief.

The two praying mantes crawled ahead, going away slowly as if the two bundles of grief on their backs were too heavy.

Father said I needed new shoes. In a few weeks we would leave the camp for America.

We went to see Grandmother's tomb, in a temple outside the refugee camp near downtown of Nongkhai province. In the temple yard, Father used a stick to brush away the leaves fallen in front of the tomb.

---

[8] Pathet Lao—Laotian People's Liberation Army, the Communists who united Laos and, later, the government.

[9] praying mantes—plural form of praying mantis, an insect that folds its front legs, as if in prayer, when it rests.

Afterwards we went downtown on foot. We stopped by a jewelry shop. From his pocket my father took out a small purse that Grandmother had put her jewelry in. From the purse he took out the pair of gold bracelets my sister wore. They must have been on her wrists when my father found her body.

"I'm comfortable in them." I peered at my toes through my sandals. "They still fit me. I need no new shoes."

But he went ahead and sold the bracelets. He then took me to a shoe shop.

I didn't want new shoes.

I had no excuse. That I had school work was not enough of a reason. My father said he scheduled the wedding on a Saturday. I had to attend it. I had no say and no choice—from the beginning I was made **mute**.[10]

My aunt and uncle picked me up in San Jose and drove me to San Francisco. We parked at Stanyan Street, next to Golden Gate Park. We crossed the street to the row of Victorian apartments.

Uncle rang the apartment doorbell while Auntie held the wedding gift. I stood behind them.

A woman in a pink dress, no doubt the bride's helper, opened the door. Her smile narrowed her eyes. She greeted us. "Come in, come in and have a seat."

We walked into the narrow hallway.

"Come, come this way." The woman led us into the living room.

I didn't know any of the guests there, a roomful. They spoke in Chinese, Lao, and English. I sat on the sofa and wondered where the bride was. I saw my father greeting the guests across the room. He wore a *complét* and a *cravat*.[11] Where did he get the suit? He looked so different—and presentable.

---

[10] **mute**—speechless; unable to speak.

[11] *complét* and a *cravat*—three-piece suit and a tie.

He came over. "You've arrived," he said.

I nodded.

He and Uncle, the two former brothers-in-law, talked as if there were no harsh feelings between them. I didn't understand how they could act so friendly to each other. Neither looked awkward or uncomfortable.

I ate candies and studied the posters on the wall— simple decoration for a wedding—the flower patterns on the drapes, the ceiling corners, the guests' faces and clothes. I parted the drapes to glance outside: the heavy traffic in the park, the sunny sky, joggers with their walkmans.

The bride in a pink gown came over to greet the guests. I wore a smile.

She looked different than she was in the refugee camp. Whenever I dropped in to see my grandmother in the hospital, I would see her across the ward tending to her bedridden father. The morning my father wrapped Grandma in a sheet of white cloth, she was present too, standing next to the coffin. And at the funeral, I spotted her in the crowd watching the smoke rising from the crematorium.[12]

"Good food," Auntie remarked to the bride. She told the bride she wanted to get the recipe for the Lao dish.

My uncle and aunt did not stay long. My father told me to go home with them because he had to stay with the guests. I left with Uncle.

Grandmother prompted me to go ahead and have dinner before it got cold. She didn't feel like eating, she said. Her eyes became red again.

My father stood outside the school, across from the hut. The sky had turned black and the dinner cold, yet he did not come in. He just stood there leaning against the post.

---

[12] crematorium—place where bodies are cremated, or burned to ashes.

Earlier Grandma had talked to him outside the hut. I had stayed in the **stilted**[13] bedroom, leaning against the bamboo wall, not daring to stir. The air was still. I heard Grandma urge my father to get married. His voice rose above hers. As his voice rose higher and higher, her sobs became harder and harder to restrain. The streaks of sunlight cast on the wall became fierce orange, then faded. Grandma had glued Thai newspapers on the walls. Mosquitoes flew around me. Grandmother came inside the hut blowing her nose with a handkerchief.

A neighbor, the French language teacher, helped Grandmother rally for marriage candidates. The teacher asked me to be nice to one of her students.

The chosen candidate was in her thirties, single and, according to herself, self-reliant.

I was polite to her, thinking that probably one day she could become my stepmother.

"I'm not thinking of marriage at the moment," she assured me. "I won't marry your father. Talk is just talk."

Her sister got caught at the Thai border and was put in prison in Bangkok.[14] The candidate needed someone who knew Thai to write to her sister. Almost every night, she stayed after her French lesson to dictate to me in Mandarin.[15] And I translated it into Thai, writing letter after letter, in the first person, asking the prisoner if she needed money, utensils, clothes, and when she would be released.

When she had no letter for me to write, the candidate stayed after class and told me about her plan to go to Canada and her progress in French and English. She talked until the light went off—the Thai administrator turning off all the light in the camp. I lighted a candle on

---

[13] **stilted**—built on supports above ground or water level.

[14] Bangkok—the capital city of Thailand.

[15] Mandarin—the official, standard spoken language of China, based on the dialect spoken in Beijing.

the table and placed it between me and her. She stayed until eleven.

Grandma's illness began.

Mother frowns, her eyebrows in a knot. It stays with her. She does not talk. She has been this way in my dreams.

I look in the mirror. I want to find her. I study my gaze and see her somewhere in my eyes. I smile and see her somewhere at the corners of my lips. The eyes smile back at me. I look more and more like my mother.

When I am by myself, she is in my silence just the way I used to see her sitting by herself in her hair parlor, in silence.

As to my sister, many times I have confused her with my half-brother in dreams. He is six now and she was about seven when she got drowned. After I wake up, I can't tell who was in my dream, whether it is my sister or my half-brother. They seem to have the same gaze and the same bright laughs, the same **prance**.[16] I wish I can tell them apart: it can be either one of them. They blend.

"Who knows what happened to her?" The anthropologist friend glanced at me. "She's in the river. For all I know, her body is rotten by now, the fish having nibbled at her, pieces of her came off."

I shut my eyes. "My mother will be hungry if there's no food for her on her death anniversary."

"There's no such thing. She will not be hungry! She's dead."

"I can feel it. There has to be food—"

"You don't do the offering for her. You do it for yourself."

"No, I do it for her sake."

"No! It's the projection of the fact that you miss her. And there's no ghost. It's merely a projection, yours."

---

[16] **prance**—spirited way of moving.

"You don't believe in spirits? Ghosts?"

"I don't like to think of my own mother as a ghost. She's not scary. She's dead but she doesn't appear as a ghost to scare her children."

"You go through the ritual yet you don't believe in it?"

"It makes me feel better."

"I'll feel better if I know for sure there's food for the dead, and they don't go hungry on their death anniversary," I said.

"If the ritual makes you feel better, then do it!"

"I haven't done any for my mother all these years."

"How about your father? Doesn't he—"

I shook my head. "He doesn't believe in it."

"See? He doesn't have the need. But you do! Let's do it this time." She asked for the date. "On that day we will perform the ritual."

"I feel phony though." I looked outside my friend's apartment window; under the overcast sky, the Bay Bridge stretching through Yerba Buena Island, toward San Francisco in the far distance. "When I kneel down to pray and bow my head, I know my mother or my grandmother does not come to the altar to take the food—since I don't see them. It sounds **hypocritical**[17] to go through the ritual—but if I don't offer the incense and food, they'll be hungry. I can feel it."

"It's not for the dead, you see. It's for yourself: you do it to put your mind at ease. The hunger is your own projection." She stopped. "Did I upset you?"

Even if I become a ghost, I would rather wander than go back to my old home. Even if I cannot find a resting place, I will not go back.

Grandma had told me that my father, when he left Laos, had turned everything over (the shop, the beds, the cabinets, everything, even family photos) to his employee. Who later got married and lived in our house.

---

[17] **hypocritical**—false; insincere.

I wonder if they (the employee and his wife and their children) still live in the house, sitting on the chairs we (the living and the dead) all used to sit on, passing through the door we passed through more than a decade ago. The same parlor. The same air.

While in other parts of the house there were cobwebs and ant trails, in the hair parlor there was none. Every morning my mother swept the floor and, holding a feather duster, dusted the recliner chair, the hair dryer, the framed black-and-white enlarged photos of my sister on the wall (the room full of images of the girl's smile), and the sewing machine with which she made my sister's and my clothes. Later in the day her friends and visitors would show up for a hairdo.

I wonder if the employee's family will realize our absence. His children must have unpacked the boxes stored in the parlor, belongings that my father couldn't take along when he fled the country for Thailand. From the boxes the children uncovered my sister's framed blowups and mother's brush, combs, hair rollers, scissors. Maybe the employee's wife had taken the brush and, after using it, left it around where she pleased.

Of course, to this family, except for the employee, there are no living and no dead, as if we'd never lived in the house.

I wonder if the dead return there, their home. I wonder if the employee's children have seen the shadows or heard some noises in the parlor, some rustling at night.

I bet my father will never go back either, even if he is free to. He cannot bear to see the house. He has given up his claim: he has a wife and two children now. And they never know the dead and gone.

QUESTIONS TO CONSIDER

1. How many specific deaths or disappearances has the narrator been forced to face?

2. Why do you think the author tells this painful story out of chronological order? What effect is created?

3. Why, at the end of the third section, does the narrator include Buddha among the "many absences"?

4. Why do you think the narrator is reluctant to attend his father's second marriage?

5. In what way does the narrator's Laotian heritage conflict with his growing American one?

6. How does the ritual on the anniversary of his mother's death help the narrator to balance two worlds?

Bowling to Find a Lost Father

BY MEE HER

Born in Laos, Mee Her came to the United States in 1976. She attended college, studied psychology, earned a master's degree and began work on her doctoral degree. In this essay, which appears in Highway 99: A Literary Journey Through California's Great Valley *(1996), the author introduces her father to bowling and having fun as a way to renew the close ties they had when she was a child.*

We all held our breath as the ball slowly rolled down the alley. Then, just as it was about to hit the pins, it dropped into the gutter. Ahhh. . . . We sighed in disappointment. My father slowly turned toward us. His eyes sparkled like those of a little boy, and a big smile was printed on his face. Then he joyfully chuckled as he walked to his seat. I never thought my father would enjoy playing with us. In fact, I never thought he'd enjoy fun. But on that evening when I taught him how to bowl,

I did more than teach him how to hit pins. I had taken the first step toward bridging a gap which had been created between him and his children.

My father had never played with us. I guess that came with his Hmong[1] orientation in valuing hard work. He told us that play was a waste of meaningful time which could be better used for productivity.

If we were still living in Laos where children don't have to go to school, and all they do is work in the field with parents, my father's orientation would be the ideal. There, children would work hard on the farms, then, during break times, they would listen to parents tell stories of their own childhood. Parents also either would teach "music" lessons to their children with instruments that they created out of bamboo sticks or they would teach them how to blow and make music out of leaves. This kept the relationship between children and their parents close. But in this country, where everything is so sophisticated, parents don't know how to be close to their children.

I remembered my relationship with my father as a child. We went everywhere together. He took me to the hospital where he worked, to the fields, or to feed the stock on the farm. I remember the times my father took me to the hospital with him. My father would teach me how his medical instruments were used, or he would show me to his patients. I felt so close to him. However, since we came to this country, my relationship with my father has changed. He no longer knows how to be the father he used to be for us. He began to build walls around us by becoming so overly protective. He did not let us play outside or go out with our friends, using concepts of hard work to keep us at home like **dutiful**[2] Hmong children. I felt emotionally distant from him.

---

[1] Hmong—relating to a people who live in the mountains of south China and the northern areas of Thailand, Vietnam, and Laos.

[2] **dutiful**—obedient; respectful.

Somehow the gap seemed so great that neither he nor his children knew how to bridge it. As it turned out, I ignored our relationship altogether.

It wasn't until my third year in college that I decided to make my first move to recreate the relationship between my father and me. I had moved away from home when I started college. The time and distance made me miss the closeness that I used to have with him. I was beginning to see the need for closeness between my parents and the other children too. My father must have tried to keep the gap from getting larger when he became overly protective of us. It must have been frightening to live with children who did not live in the same world that he did. He couldn't play video games with them and couldn't understand ear-busting rock 'n roll. He didn't even know how to play soccer or volleyball! And those were the things that his children did for enjoyment in this country.

Poor Dad. It was not his fault that he did not know how to be included in our lives. It was just that he didn't know how to get involved with his children. That was why my brothers and sisters and I decided to introduce my father to bowling.

I remember that day well when my brother, sisters, dad, and I went bowling. Dad was a little hesitant to come with us, but we all persuaded him. When we got to the bowling alley, we showed him how to hold the ball. Then we taught him how to throw the ball. It was a little bit foreign for me to be the one teaching my father, and I sensed that Father felt odd, too. But once he got the hang of it, he did well. He even made a couple of strikes![3]

I think it was much more than bowling that father enjoyed. It was the emotional closeness that he felt with us which made him come back to bowl again. The next time we went bowling, he was teaching the younger

---

[3] strikes—in bowling, a strike occurs when all the bowling pins are knocked down by one roll of the ball.

children to bowl. As I watched him beam so happily with the kids, it occurred to me that this was the beginning of building a bridge across a long-created gap between Dad and his children. Another thought came to my mind too. I wonder why it had taken me so long to show my father how to bowl. Was I waiting for him to make the first move? Was I waiting for him to teach me instead? But how could he have done that when he didn't know how?

QUESTIONS TO CONSIDER

1. How does the father's profession and role in the family change after coming to the United States?

2. What causes the gap between the father and his children?

3. What does Mee Her mean when she says, "But in this country, where everything is so sophisticated, parents don't know how to be close to their children"? What do you think of her statement?

4. How does being away at college help Mee Her to understand her relationship with her father in a way that she couldn't see when she was at home?

5. How does the parent and child relationship change in this family's move to a new country? What challenges can this change present for both parents and children?

6. How does the bowling alley help Mee balance her two worlds? Are there some other ways she might have accomplished the same thing?

Yo-Yo Ma

BY MARINA MA

as told to John A. Rallo

*Marina Ma is the mother of world-renowned Chinese-American
cellist Yo-Yo Ma, who was born in Paris, France, in 1955 and moved
with his family to the United States in 1961. He decided upon the
cello as his instrument at the age of four, and the following year
he gave his first recitals, first in Paris and then in New York. A student
whom the famed cellist Pablo Casals encouraged, Yo-Yo Ma received
the prestigious Avery Fisher Award in 1978 and a Grammy Award in
1985. These excerpts from* My Son, Yo-Yo *(1995) show readers
the meeting of Eastern and Western influences in a stunning
account of this "classical music superstar."*

> *"Child prodigies[1] are still perceived as unexplained and somehow unnatural occurrences, and they have been greeted over the generations with an ambivalent[2] mix of emotions that accompany the expectation of change: fear and wariness, mystery and myth, skepticism and contempt, awe and wonder."*

David Henry Feldman, **Nature's Gambit**

Marina[3] wondered about the little signs she saw in her son and was perplexed. His behavior did not fit into the mold generally associated with the normal development of a child. Her experience with other so-called child prodigies was limited, but in her mother's heart she knew that Yo-Yo was "different." She also knew that all parents are convinced that their children are exceptional when they show remarkable skills or behave in a manner far beyond their ages. She realized Yo-Yo was talented, but she also realized that talent alone was not sufficient to insure success in his particular field.

. . .

From the cradle, Yo-Yo was surrounded by a world of music; he heard hundreds of classical selections on records, or played by his father or his sister. Bach and Mozart were engraved in his mind.

From his mother, a former opera singer, he inherited a love for song and always sang in tune. His notes were clear and never sharp or flat.

Wondering how her two-year-old child could explain that the pitch was too high or too low, she questioned him. With childish simplicity he would reply "Mommy, I don't know. I just know."

---

[1] *prodigies*—exceptionally talented people.

[2] *ambivalent*—made up of opposite attitudes or feelings.

[3] While Marina Ma is the "author" of this piece, she did not write it. She told her story to John A. Rallo. He writes about her, therefore, in the third person, not the first-person "I."

Yo-Yo was unaware of this unique gift, but his mother suspected that her son's talent for music was something special, something to be reckoned with, and when she told her husband, he had to agree.

Destiny had placed a gifted child in their care and it was their responsibility not to let it go to waste. Yo-Yo's talent awed them; finding the right key to channel that talent, that potential to music greatness posed a serious challenge. They thought of their own poverty and their own struggle to survive in the highly competitive field of music. Did they dare direct him on the same road they had traveled?

"Let's just wait and see what life holds, how things develop," Marina suggested. "We'll make music just a part of his education; we'll not try to influence him in any way to become a professional musician."

Marina felt that once motivated, a child would go on his own, whether at school, at games with toys, or in any other endeavor.

"You want Yo-Yo to play a string instrument?" she said to her husband. "Very well, let him become interested, and we'll see what happens."

Dr. Ma listened to his wife's rationalization. He listened but remained unconvinced by her words. He had always maintained that it took three generations to produce a good musician. The first generation provided the funds; the second profited from the money by receiving the best education possible, and the third attained the goal set, provided that the right combination of genes was present.

For Hiao-Tsiun Ma,[4] that theory rang true: his father, a wealthy landlord, had provided the necessary funds for him to receive an excellent education. Yo-Yo was the third generation.

But was it fair to impose his dream on his son?

---

[4] Hiao-Tsiun Ma—Marina's husband, Yo-Yo's father.

*   *   *

Marina finished washing the dinner dishes and was sponging off the table. Her husband looked up at her from behind his thick, **concave**[5] lenses bordered by a silver frame.

"You're right. Our child is very gifted," he began in his calm way. Without mincing words, he announced, "I'm going to make a musician of him."

This sudden **revelation**[6] did not surprise her, although she wished it would have never come. She knew her husband well, and from past little hints here and there, she suspected that it was just a matter of time when he would do what he always wanted. It couldn't have been otherwise. Still, she made one last attempt.

"Look," she said, "look how hard our lives have been. We both have studied music and pray tell me, where has it got us? We can't even make ends meet."

His face remained impassive.

Appealing to his father's pride, she added, "Do you want our son to suffer the same fate as ours?"

The rhetorical question[7] missed its mark.

For the time being, he went on quietly.

After the crowded condition in their one-room quarters, they considered themselves fortunate to enjoy the luxury of their two-room apartment. Mother and children slept in one room; the other, a smaller bedroom-studio was used by Hiao-Tsiun. Amazingly he had squeezed into that room his piano, a collection of children's string instruments, and his cot. His precious manuscripts and music scores, meticulously arranged by him for children, were jammed into an old armoire[8] and piled up on the piano top. Every corner was bulging with his papers.

---

[5] **concave**—cupped, rounded inward.

[6] **revelation**—announcement; disclosure.

[7] A rhetorical question is asked for effect only; no answer is required or expected.

[8] armoire—tall cupboard or wardrobe.

Though it was small, Dr. Ma felt comfortable in it. It was his inner sanctum.

In the days that followed, Marina went about her household duties. His decision had left her in a **quandary**.[9] Was her husband right in persisting? On the other hand, she could not forget the scene that had transpired between Yo-Yo and Yeou-Cheng after her first concert at the University of Paris. Here was a seven-and-a-half-year-old performer asking her little brother, "Well, did you like it? How well did I play?"

Yo-Yo looked at her, his black eyes lighting up. "Sis, dear Sis, you played very well . . . " He hesitated for a moment, measuring his words. "You were great. But . . . But you were just a little off tone . . ."

Marina marveled at her son's **diplomatic**[10] way of offering criticism, being careful of his sister's feelings. He was only three years old!

Yeou-Cheng, accepting his observation with curiosity, persisted, "How much off tone was I?" To which he quickly replied in French, *Une petite virgule*—just a little comma."

The amazing thing about it all was that Yo-Yo was not familiar with a single note of that musical selection!

From that time forth, Yo-Yo would act as Yeou-Cheng's "press agent" every time she performed.

In the lobby he counted people as they arrived and reported back to his sister with great excitement, so much was his delight in her success.

Yo-Yo was alive with life, always ready to say and do something to make others happy. After all, his name meant "friend."

In spite of all the positive signs Yo-Yo was showing, Marina kept making all sorts of excuses for not wanting a musical career for her son. And when Hiao-Tsiun

---

[9] **quandary**—state of puzzlement or doubt.
[10] **diplomatic**—tactful.

plagued her with "think it over, think of the injustice we may do him if we do not at least try," she would reply, "That's just it; I am thinking of him."

Her heart beat with a different beat from her husband's, yet she was filled with a sense of guilt.

Marina thought it was enough for Yo-Yo to be studying piano, but since Yeou-Cheng had already begun playing a second instrument—a violin—why should she deny the same opportunity to her son? After all, his father could teach him too, using the small-sized violin, which Yeou-Cheng had outgrown and all the music sheets. It would be like a younger child inheriting an older brother's or sister's clothes.

To his father, however, it was evident that Yo-Yo had no real interest in playing the violin, although he was very good at it.

Dr. Ma was perplexed. It was against his **pedagogical**[11] theory to force a child to make music; he had to do it because he liked it. The problem was resolved when little Yo-Yo said to him, "I don't like the sound violins make; I want a big instrument."

To encourage his gifted son, Dr. Ma said to him, "I'll get one for you, one way or another." But he admonished, "Mind you, once you start with a big instrument, you cannot switch back to the violin. Don't tell me a month from now that you have changed your mind."

Yo-Yo, familiar with the firm tone in his father's voice, knew he meant every word. "I will play it," he stated resolutely. "I won't change my mind."

Patiently, Dr. Ma improvised a "big instrument" by attaching an end pin[12] to a viola. After all, that should satisfy a three-year old. So he thought. But Yo-Yo knew

---

[11] **pedagogical**—educational.

[12] end pin—slender post attached to the bottom of a cello to hold it firmly in place on the floor. By attaching an end pin to a viola, an instrument slightly larger than a violin that is held under the chin, Dr. Ma thought he could satisfy his son's desire for a "big instrument."

better and proved it at the Conservatory concert he attended with his father.

Yo-Yo sat completely absorbed in what he heard, but especially in what he saw. "I want *that*," he told his father, jumping from his seat as he pointed to a big double-bass on the stage.

"You don't want *that*; it's too big for you. You won't be able to hold it."

Yo-Yo avoided the issue. He knew exactly what he wanted and was bent on getting it.

Struck by the intensity of the request and wanting to make his son happy, especially since he was showing so much self-motivation and determination, Dr. Ma was inclined to go along. Still, he worried lest Yo-Yo might change his mind. He was but a mere child.

He decided to allow a few months to go by, hoping that the matter would be forgotten. But Yo-Yo, persistent, kept reminding him, "When am I going to get the 'big instrument'?"

Partly because of Yo-Yo's insistence, partly because he had faith in his son's promising future, Dr. Ma went to see Monsieur Vatelot, one of Paris's foremost violin makers, for advice.

"Let him have it; I know Yo-Yo. He will give you no peace until he holds a 'big instrument' in his hands." Besides, he added, "I have a feeling it is a sign that something good will come out of it."

They decided upon a cello.

Marina, of course, had been kept in the dark about all these goings-on until her husband brought home the 1/16th cello Monsieur Vatelot had loaned him. That was the last straw for Marina. There was nothing more she could say or do. If that is what my husband wants, all well and good, she thought. Let him pay for the consequences of his actions.

Yo-Yo, of course, was ecstatic and jumped with joy. A 1/16th cello looked very big to a tiny boy.

. . .

Yo-Yo possessed a formidable and uncanny power of concentration, **indispensable**[13] to his training. Training alone, however, does not a "boy wonder" make in the world of music. What helped the training along was his **insatiable**[14] curiosity to learn and achieve—a curiosity that has stayed with him throughout his life.

. . .

Cello lessons continued. Having given Yo-Yo the best of his musical expertise, Dr. Ma knew the time had come to seek out more renowned teachers for further studies. That is what he had done with Yeou-Cheng when he took her to Belgium for violin lessons with the highly respected Arthur Grumiaux. He did the same for Yo-Yo, selecting Mme. Michelle Lepinte, a well-known cello instructor.

Before taking Yo-Yo to Mme. Lepinte, Dr. Ma had used études by Bach for his son's lessons, spending countless hours preparing arrangements and listening patiently while he practiced.

When Mme. Lepinte found out, she frowned upon the choice of composer. "Dr. Ma," she said to him, "Why have you chosen Bach for Yo-Yo? He's much too difficult for a child that age."

When Dr. Ma made no reply, she thought it best not to pursue the matter further.

There was no question in Hiao-Tsiun's mind that Yo-Yo could easily accomplish the task by learning only two measures of the music each day. By the second day, he would know four measures. By the third day, he would know six measures, and so on.

When he thought his son ready, he sprang a surprise for Mme. Lepinte, by asking Yo-Yo to play the entire

---

[13] **indespensable**—essential; required.

[14] **insatiable**—inability to be satisfied.

Bach piece. She was dazzled. Never in her long years of teaching had she heard anything like it. The performer was Yo-Yo, but she knew that it was his father's method that had triumphed.

When Yo-Yo was not yet six years old, he was making his début with the same Bach Suite plus a selection from a composition by Paul Bazelaire. Before the concert, however, Yo-Yo told his father that he was going to play "the whole thing," by which he meant the entire eight parts of the composition. His father reminded him that the program listed him as playing one or two selections only. But nothing could **dissuade**[15] Yo-Yo.

"You can't do that," his father retorted, "if you play the entire suite, it will take much longer than the time they allotted you on the program. The audience will then say, What kind of parents are we to make a child study so hard? They would not think kindly of us; they would have the impression that we are heartless."

Yo-Yo was quick to understand his father's concern and, of course, would do nothing to cause him pain or embarrassment. He reflected for a few seconds, his mind working at great speed.

"Bien," he said. "O.K. I have an idea." And he went on to outline his strategy.

"When I finish playing the first part," he began, "you applaud. The audience will follow your applause. Then I will play the second part. When I finish, you'll applaud again. And each time I finish another part, you'll applaud again, until the entire eight parts have been played. Each time you applaud, the audience will follow with their applause. In that way, the people can't blame you for letting me play the whole thing, for I would be playing in response to their applause."

He played for almost an hour, and at the end, the audience went wild with applause and shouts of "Bravo!"

---

[15] **dissuade**—discourage; deter.

"Imagine," Marina recalled, "this was the way Yo-Yo's mind worked—quick like a flash." Then, smiling, she added, "His stubborn streak never left him."

Dr. Ma was well aware that prodigies cannot be created. They can be directed, they can be refined, they can be polished—but the source of genius must be there at birth. Some are discovered; others are "born to blush unseen," as a poet once wrote. Part of Yo-Yo's training may have advanced through discipline, but deep in his heart, Yo-Yo loved music and strove to achieve beyond his years, beyond the instruction he received. He practiced his music dutifully and when praised for the "work-out," he was as happy as any other child who received a pat on the head.

* * *

Was it Destiny or was it his father's will that Yo-Yo became a cello virtuoso? No one will ever know. Certainly it did not just happen. His parents' cultural background was bound to rub off on him. And that too, made a difference.

The language Yo-Yo first heard and learned from his parents was Chinese. In Paris, however, he was exposed to another language. This cultural duality made him aware of his own ethnic background, which stressed obedience, hard-work, endurance, patience and discipline. As he grew older, he could never forget his bi-cultural upbringing, which played such a major role in the development of his personality.

* * *

It is said that musicians are born and that talents are made. The truism clearly applies to Yo-Yo. Thanks to the family into which he was born, he was destined to shine from the very beginning. The music that flows from his cello is the voice of his soul; the language it speaks is the universal language understood by the mind and felt by the heart. Isaac Stern, who first heard Yo-Yo play at the age of five and who invited him in later years to become a regular participant in the now well known chamber music **ensemble**,[16] "Isaac Stern and Friends," maintained that one had "to have the bow arm be the guide, but to let his ears become the motivation factor." Yo-Yo learned to do just that.

In pleasing his own ear, Yo-Yo has also succeeded in pleasing the ear of his listeners, who, as Marina expressed in her own simple way, interact with him, "The audience is one with him; when he breathes, the audience also breathes; when he stops, the audience also stops. As Yo-Yo becomes absorbed in his music, so does the audience. It isn't how far the audience takes him, but how far he takes the audience with his playing. It is that special, magic moment when artist and audience are **fused**[17] into one. Ever since childhood, Yo-Yo has had this power to attract people and move them. He is happy when others share his feelings for music and he revels in that moment of ecstasy when the audience forgets itself and is transported by the sheer beauty of sound. For Yo-Yo has that consummate gift to penetrate the mind and the heart of the composer and transmit that feeling to the audience, who is in total harmony with him."

Music critics have not failed to acknowledge this audience reaction. William Mootz wrote:

> This youthful Chinese-American galloped on stage with a smile that could have melted icebergs. Before he played a note, he had his audience captivated. When he drew his bow across his instrument a few minutes later, he had us all **mesmerized**.[18]

---

[16] **ensemble**—group.

[17] **fused**—blended thoroughly as if melted together.

[18] **mesmerized**—spellbound; enthralled.

Did Marina, who had trained as an opera singer, coach her son on his stage presence? She denied it. Nevertheless, his body movements suggest "stage" directions. She added that they were natural with Yo-Yo; he was always a keen observer. "The movements are not rehearsed nor are they mere frills; in his case, they help to enhance his technique. If an opera singer wants to project her voice far," she explained, "accompanying gestures help her reach the audience, 'drawing' it into the act. That is precisely the point of a performer: he 'pulls in' the public. With his particular technique and spontaneous movements, Yo-Yo's cello projects its 'voice' far. The audience, captivated, is moved emotionally."

On stage, Yo-Yo offers joy, excitement and rapture, which linger long after the performance has ended. His manner of playing bonds him to the spectators and a spiritual **communion**[19] takes place "lifting them onto the stage and onto him." Were this not so, one could easily listen to his recordings.

. . .

Yo-Yo is a superstar now. His achievements, however, did not result without hard, sustained work. He plays effortlessly, without thinking of notes. Undoubtedly, his mastery of Bach *études* at an early age, which his father insisted that he learn, contributed greatly to the technique which he has developed.

Yo-Yo's selection as the sole recipient of the prestigious Avery Fisher Prize in 1978, his subsequent honorary degrees from Harvard, Yale and other universities, and his appearances as guest artist with major orchestras, including the New York Philharmonic, the Chicago Symphony, the Boston and Philadelphia Orchestras, the Los Angeles Philharmonic, and the Chamber Music Society of Lincoln Center in the United

---

[19] **communion**—synergy; spirit of connection and closeness.

States and with the English Chamber Orchestra, the Berlin Philharmonic, the Royal Philharmonic, the Orchestre Nationale de France, the Israel Philharmonic, and the Vienna Philharmonic overseas attest to the prominence he enjoys in classical music. Most of all, his prankish sense of humor, his sparkling personality, his generosity and his love "to make music" for audiences the world over continue to endear him to all.

QUESTIONS TO CONSIDER

1. In what ways did Yo-Yo demonstrate his special musical talent at a very young age?

2. Why did Yo-Yo's mother, Marina, worry about encouraging her son to become a musician?

3. In what ways did Yo-Yo's parents' cultural background "rub off" on their son?

4. How does Yo-Yo's playing affect his audience, and why is listening to him in a live performance different from listening to a recording?

5. What aspects of Yo-Yo's pursuit of his special musical talent can be generalized to dreams and talents by anyone in any area of interest?

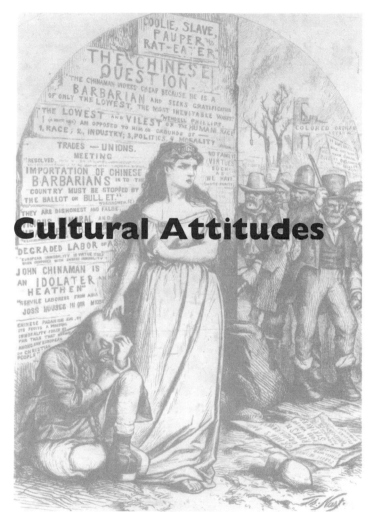

▲

The Chinese Question Anti-Chinese slurs displayed on the wall in Thomas Nast's ugly cartoon reflect the prejudice that led to the Chinese Exclusion Act of 1882. It shows the figure of Liberty protecting a Chinese immigrant from an angry mob.

▲

"Exotic Oriental" In the early part of the twentieth century, American popular culture frequently depicted Chinese as exotic villains. In this scene the legendary Myrna Loy (not of Asian heritage) plays the title character in *The Daughter of Fu Manchu.*

▲
"Threat to Society" Fear and racial stereotyping led to the internment of Japanese Americans living on the West Coast during World War II.

▲

Celebrating Tradition Women from India perform in their traditional dresses, called *saris*, at an Indian cultural festival in Edison, New Jersey.

▲
A Welcome Sign A sign in New York City displays the street's name in Chinese characters. The translation is a useful aid for recent immigrants who do not yet read English and an indication of the city's willingness to accommodate their needs.

▲
Embracing Different Worlds Chinatowns, like this one in Los Angeles, California, are popular places for people of all ethnic backgrounds to gather, eat, and shop.

▲

International Film Star Jackie Chan (right) laughs with fellow actor Wesley Snipes (middle) and Hong Kong publisher Curtis Wong (left) before being presented with an award honoring his positive portrayals of Asian Americans.

▲

Celebrating Multicultural Diversity Famed chef Wolfgang Puck and architectural designer Barbara Lazaroff welcome guests to their new restaurant, Chinois, in 1998 in Las Vegas. (*Chinois* is the French word for China.) The trendy eatery is one of a growing number of restaurants to integrate Asian, European, and American cuisines.

ACKNOWLEDGEMENTS

Texts

12 Abridgment of "Immigration Blues" from *Songs of Gold Mountain: Cantonese Rhymes from San Francisco Chinatown* by Marlon K. Hom. Copyright © 1987 The Regents of the University of California. Reprinted by permission.

16 From *Homebase* by Shawn Wong. Copyright © Shawn Hsu Wong. Used by permission of Dutton Signet, a division of Penguin Putnam Inc.

21 Excerpt from *America Is in the Heart: A Personal History* by Carlos Bulosan, copyright 1946 by Harcourt, Inc., reprinted by permission of the publisher.

26 Excerpt from "Of Luggage and Shoes" by Thuy Dinh in *Once Upon A Dream...* edited by DeTran, Andrew Lam, and Hai Dai Nguyen. Copyright © 2000 San Jose Mercury News. Used with permission.

32 "Song of Calling Souls" reprinted from *Of Flesh & Spirit*, © 1998 by Wang Ping, with permission from Coffee House Press.

42 From "In the American Society" by Gish Jen. Copyright © 1986 by Gish Jen. First published in *Southern Review*. Reprinted by permission of the author.

56 "Appendix A: A Chronology of Asian American History" by Judy Yung from *Making Waves* by Asian Women United of California. © 1989 by Asian Women United of California. Reprinted by permission of Beacon Press, Boston.

74 From *Quiet Odyssey: A Pioneer Korean Woman in America* by Mary Paik Lee, edited with an introduction by Sucheng Chan. Copyright © 1990 by the University of Washington Press. Reprinted by permission of the University of Washington Press.

82 Excerpt from *Farewell To Manzanar* by James D. and Jeanne Wakatsuki Houston. Copyright © 1973 by James D. Houston. Reprinted by permission of Houghton Mifflin Co. All rights reserved.

96 From *No-No Boy* by John Okada. Copyright © 1976 by Dorothy Okada. Reprinted by permission of the University of Washington Press.

103 Excerpted and reprinted from "Working and Dealing with Racism in San Diego" by Juanita Santos included in *Filipino American Lives* by Yen Le Espiritu, by permission of Temple University Press. © 1995 by Temple University. All rights reserved.

105 Excerpted and reprinted from "Discrimination in San Diego" by Connie Tirona included in *Filipino American Lives* by Yen Le Espiritu, by permission of Temple University Press. © 1995 by Temple University. All rights reserved.

118 From *The Floating World* by Cynthia Kadohata, copyright © 1989 Cynthia Kadohata. Used by permission of Viking Penguin Inc.

127 From *Vedi* by Ved Mehta (New York: W.W. Norton, 1987) Copyright © 1981 by Ved Mehta. First appeared in *The New Yorker.* Reprinted by permission of Georges Borchardt, Inc., for the author.

138 Mirikitani, Janice. "Ms." excerpted from *We, the Dangerous: New and Selected Poems*, copyright © 1995 by Janice Mirikitani. Reprinted by permission of Celestial Arts, P.O. Box 7123, Berkeley, CA 94707.

141 From *China Boy* by Gus Lee, copyright © 1991 Augustus S.M.S. Lee. Used by permission of Dutton, a division of Penguin Putnam Inc.

145 "My Mother Juggling Bean Bags" by James Masao Mitsui. Reprinted by permission of the author.

148 "The Lemon Tree Billiards House." Copyright © by Cedric Yamanaka. Reprinted by permission of the author.

164 "On Being Asian American" by Lawson Fusao Inada. Copyright © by Lawson F. Inada. Reprinted by permission of the author.

167 From *The Woman Warrior* by Maxine Hong Kingston. Copyright © 1975, 1976 by Maxine Hong Kingston. Reprinted by permission of Alfred A. Knopf, a division of Random House Inc.

172 "Lost Sister" by Cathy Song from *Picture Bride*, 1983. Reprinted by permission of Yale University Press.

176 "Mother Tongue" by Amy Tan. First published in *The Threepenny Review*. Copyright © 1990 by Amy Tan. Reprinted by permission of the author and the Sandra Dijkstra Literary Agency.

185 "Those Years" by T.C. Huo, *Seattle Review,* 1988. Reprinted by permission of the Seattle Review.

196 "Bowling to Find a Lost Father" by Mee Her from *Passages: An Anthology of the Southeast Asian Refugee Experience* compiled by Katsuyo Howard.

200 Reprinted with permission by The Chinese University Press from *My Son, Yo-Yo* by Marina Ma, 1995.

Photo Research Diane Hamilton.

Photos 65, 66, 109 *bottom,* **110** *bottom,* **111, 114, 115** © Bettmann/ CORBIS;
67, 213, 215 Courtesy of the Library of Congress; **68** © L Dematteis/
The Image Works, Inc.; **69–71, 116, 137** *bottom,* **218–219** © AP/Wide
World Photos; **72** © Louise Gubb/The Image Works, Inc.; **108** © Steve
McCutcheon/Visuals Unlimited; **109** *top* © David Sams/Stock Boston;
110 *top* © Schermeister/CORBIS; **112** © Matthew Borkoski/Index;
113 *top* © Len Rubenstein/Index Stock Imagery; **113** *bottom* Omni Photo
Communications Inc./Index Stock Imagery; **134** © Jerry Bauer
Photography; **135** © Mary Levin/Shawn Wong; **136** *top* © James D.
Wilson/Liaison Agency; **136** *bottom* © John Chiasson/Liaison Agency;
137 *top* © Courtesy of the University of Washington; **214** © Kobal
Collection; **216** © Rudi Von Briel/PhotoEdit; **217** *top* © Robert Brenner/
PhotoEdit; **217** *bottom* © Phil Borden/PhotoEdit.

*Every effort has been made to secure complete rights and permissions for each
selection presented herein. Updated acknowledgements, if needed, will appear in
subsequent printings.*

Index

Los Gatos High School